# GRAINS

MIRIAM RUBIN

PHOTOGRAPHY BY

DANA GALLAGHER

CollinsPublishersSanFrancisco

*A Division of* HarperCollins*Publishers*

First published in USA 1995 by Collins Publishers San Francisco
1160 Battery Street, San Francisco, CA 94111

PRODUCED BY SMALLWOOD & STEWART, INC., NEW YORK CITY

© 1995 Smallwood & Stewart, Inc.

EDITOR: David Ricketts
FOOD STYLING: Anne Disrude
BOOK DESIGN: Susi Oberhelman
DESIGN ASSISTANT: Pat Tan

Library of Congress Cataloging-in-Publication Data

    Rubin, Miriam.
       Grains / Miriam Rubin.
          p.      cm. — (The gourmet pantry)
       Includes index.
       ISBN 0-00-225210-4
       1. Cookery (Cereals)    2. Grain.    I. Title.    II. Series.
    TX808.R83   1995
    641.6'31—dc20                    95-5951

PRINTED IN ITALY

10 9 8 7 6 5 4 3 2 1

# CONTENTS

# INTRODUCTION

Grains have always been an essential part of our diet. Consider the oatmeal we eat for breakfast, the bread in the ham on rye sandwich we grab for lunch, the cookie we munch after dinner—all of these are made from different grains.

Beyond that familiar bowl of oatmeal, there are enormous possibilities for grains. In these pages there are rich, satisfying soups and light salads, warming stews and delicious main dishes, with meat and without. Here, grains even star in desserts.

As with different vegetables, each grain is unique, each with a character of its own, which can take wonderfully to different preparations and flavorings, from sweet to savory.

Each has its own distinctive flavor—some strong, like rye, others more mellow and less assertive, like barley and oats. Some are sweet and rich-tasting—for example, millet and cornmeal—and some are earthy, such as buckwheat, wheat berries, kamut, and spelt. Some grains are quick to cook, others take more time. Cornmeal, quinoa, and millet are all done in about 20 minutes. Wheat berries take about 1½ hours but need little attention;

because they keep well, prepare more than you need and refrigerate the rest for a salad, or stir into a soup or stew.

Grains are not only versatile and varied, they are also a marvelous source of nutrition. Under the inedible husk of each grain kernel is the bran, a source of dietary fiber, as well as vitamins and minerals. Beneath that is the germ, rich in enzymes, proteins, minerals, fat, and vitamins. Inside the germ is the heart of the grain, the endosperm, which contains carbohydrates.

To get the most flavor and nutritional benefit, use grains in a form that is processed the least, depending on the recipe, of course. Choose old-fashioned rolled oats rather than quick-cooking and old-fashioned grits rather than instant. When making polenta, look for coarse-ground cornmeal instead of instant polenta, or opt for a stone-ground meal, which contains the germ. Most grains are easily found in your local market. More unusual grains, such as amaranth and quinoa, and less processed forms of grains are found at health-food stores. Try to buy grains from a busy store that has a quick turnover, and keep them in airtight containers in a cool, dry place: Whole-grain flours and meals are happiest in the refrigerator or freezer.

The recipes that follow only begin to explore the potential of grains. May you enjoy them and discover your own ways to prepare this under-appreciated staple.

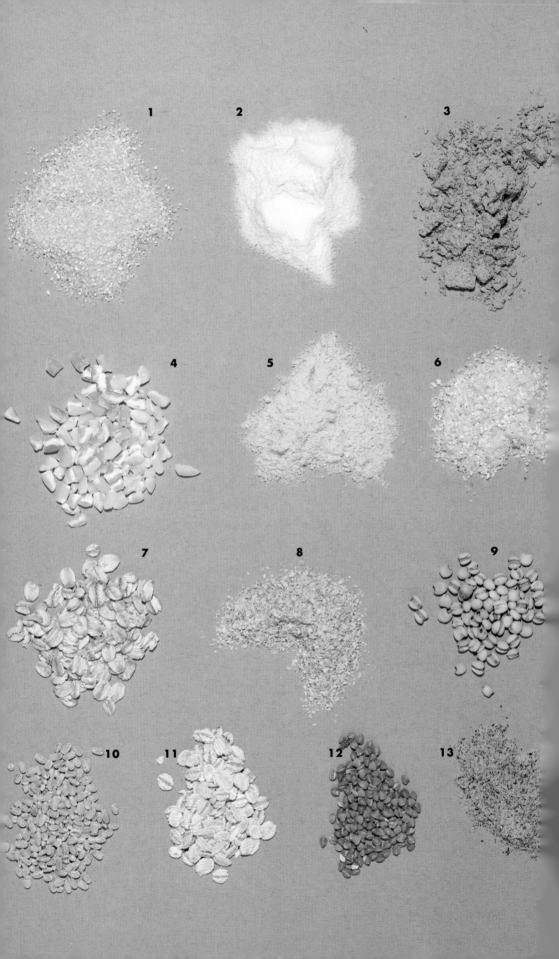

# GLOSSARY

**AMARANTH (21)**

An ancient Aztec grain. Tiny, gold-colored with black flecks, amaranth is high in protein and vitamins, with a crunchy texture and peppery flavor. Available whole, ground into flour, puffed, and processed into pasta and cereal.

**BARLEY (9, 10, 11)**

One of the first known plants. Beige and shaped like a flattened oval, barley is usually sold pearled (hulled and polished to cook more quickly). Other forms are: quick-cooking, whole hulled barley, Job's tears (large hulled grains), grits, flakes, and flour.

**BRAN**

The outer layer of the kernel of the grain once the husk has been removed. An excellent source of fiber, vitamins, and minerals.

**BUCKWHEAT (13)**

Triangular seeds from a fruit related to rhubarb and sorrel, it has a nutty flavor and is sold roasted (kasha), whole grain, or cracked, or unroasted in groat, grits, or ground into flour.

**BULGUR (15, 18)**

Wheat kernels that have been steamed, dried, and cracked. Often it is not cooked at all but soaked until tender. It is sold in fine, medium, and coarse granulations. Do not substitute cracked wheat.

**CORN**

The kernels that grow on the ear of the corn plant. They are generally yellow, white, or bi-colored; other varieties range from red to blue to black. The type we eat on or off the cob is sweet corn.

**CORNMEAL (1, 2, 3, 5)**

Corn kernels, either white, yellow, or blue, that have been dried and ground. Available ground fine, medium, or coarse.

**COUSCOUS**

Not a grain, but a tiny pasta made from ground semolina wheat, couscous is often treated like a grain. It is sold in regular and quick-cooking varieties.

**FLOUR**

A fine meal made by grinding grains, "flour" usually refers to a flour made of wheat. All-purpose flour, a blend of hard and soft wheats, is used most often.

**GRAIN**

The edible seeds, or kernels, of cereal grass. Each kernel has four layers. The outer layer is the husk, which is not eaten. Beneath that is the bran, which surrounds the germ. Finally, there is the endosperm, the heart of the kernel. White flour is made from the finely ground endosperm, from which all the nutritious bran and germ have been removed.

## GRITS (6)

Usually refers to hominy grits, which are made from coarsely ground, hulled, dried corn kernels. Grits can also be made from other grains, such as oats or barley.

## GROATS

Refers both to whole hulled grains and to hulled grains that have been cracked. Cracked groats are coarser in texture than grits.

## HOMINY, WHOLE (4)

Whole white, yellow, or black corn kernels, treated with lime, lye, or other caustic substances to loosen the hulls and partially cook the kernels, then washed and dried. It is sold dried or fully cooked and canned. Called *posole* in Spanish.

## HOMINY GRITS

Dried white or yellow corn kernels that have been ground to a coarse, medium, or fine texture.

## KAMUT (24)

An ancient variety of high-protein wheat, with large kernels and an oval shape. Available whole, or processed into pastas and cereals.

## KASHA (12)

Roasted buckwheat groats, sold whole or cracked in coarse, medium, or fine grain (see *Buckwheat*).

## MEAL

Coarsely ground grain, ground finer than grits but not as fine as flour.

## MILLET (23)

A highly nutritious, mild, sweet-flavored grain. Round and golden yellow, millet is sold whole (hulls removed), ground into a coarse meal, ground into flour, or puffed for cereal.

## OATS (7, 8)

A protein-rich grain usually eaten as a hot cereal or in prepared cereals. Available forms: whole hulled groats; steel-cut (Scottish) oats; rolled oats, which are steamed groats that have been flattened with rollers (quick-cooking oats are rolled oats that have been further cut and processed); oat bran; and oat flour.

## POSOLE (4)

See *Hominy, Whole*.

## QUINOA (22)

An ancient Incan staple. Pronounced *keen*-wah, this tiny, flat, off-white seed is not a true grain, but the fruit of an herb in the goosefoot family. Mild-flavored and crunchy, quinoa is one of the best grain-based sources of protein, calcium, and iron. It is sold in whole-grain form, ground into flour, and processed into pasta. Rinse for 2 minutes before using to remove the saponin, a natural bitter-tasting coating.

## RYE (14)

Mainly used as a flour for bread-making. Rye is high in protein yet low in gluten. Available forms: rye berries, rye grits, rye meal, rye flour, and rye flakes.

## SPELT

A large, brown, oval grain of an ancient variety of wheat with a nutty flavor. It is sold whole, rolled into flakes, ground into flour, and processed into pasta. Spelt can often be tolerated by people with wheat allergies.

## WHEAT (16, 17, 19, 20)

Our most important grain, and one of the oldest grains cultivated. Available forms: berries (whole, hulled kernels), cracked wheat, bulgur, grits, shredded wheat, unprocessed bran (or miller's bran), wheat germ, rolled wheat flakes, puffed wheat, cream of wheat, and wheat flour.

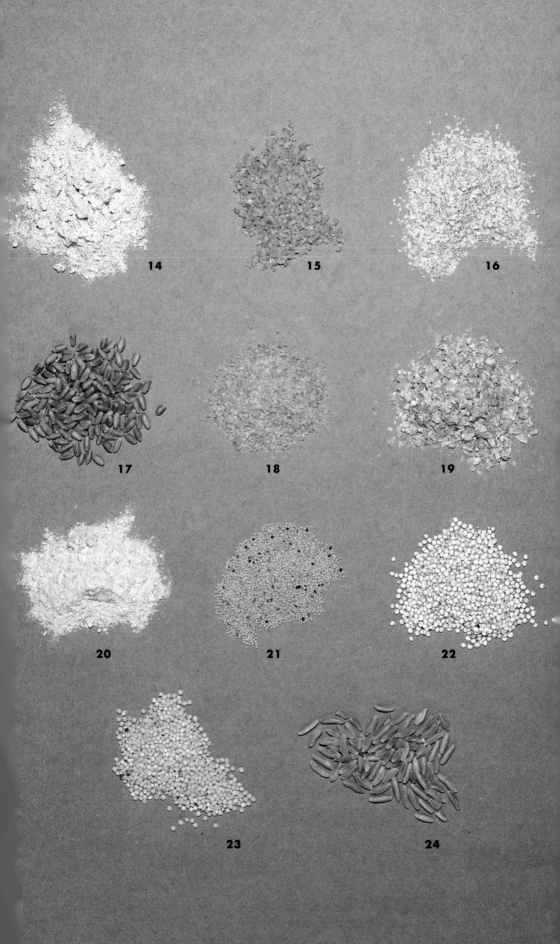

# TOMATO SOUP WITH QUINOA & PESTO

THIS EASY, FLAVORFUL SOUP IS PERFECT FOR
A LIGHT LUNCH, YET ELEGANT ENOUGH
FOR A DINNER PARTY. QUINOA ADDS A PLEASANT
TEXTURE AND CRUNCH TO THE SOUP,
WHICH CONTRASTS WITH THE CREAMY PESTO.

In a heavy small nonreactive saucepan, combine the quinoa, ⅔ cup water, and the salt and bring to a boil over high heat. Reduce the heat to low, cover, and simmer for 15 to 20 minutes, or until the water is absorbed and the grains are translucent and begin to uncoil. Set the saucepan aside, covered.

Meanwhile, in a food processor fitted with the metal blade, process the tomatoes with their purée until almost smooth.

In a heavy large saucepan, heat the oil over medium-high heat. Stir in the onions, garlic, pepper, and sugar and sauté for 5 to 6 minutes, or until the onions are tender and light golden.

Stir in the puréed tomatoes and broth. Increase the heat to high and bring to a boil. Reduce the heat to medium-low and simmer, uncovered, stirring occasionally, for 15 minutes, or until the soup is slightly thickened.

Meanwhile, prepare the pesto: In a food processor fitted with the metal blade, combine the basil, Parmesan, oil, broth, sour cream, and garlic and process to a smooth purée.

To serve, fluff the quinoa with a fork and stir into the soup. Ladle the soup into warmed bowls and top each serving with about 1 tablespoon of the pesto, swirling the pesto through the soup. Garnish with basil sprigs, if desired.

⅓ cup quinoa, rinsed for 2 minutes

⅛ teaspoon salt

1 (28-ounce) can whole tomatoes in purée

2 tablespoons extra-virgin olive oil

1½ cups chopped white onions

2 garlic cloves, minced

½ teaspoon freshly ground black pepper

¼ teaspoon sugar

2 cups chicken broth

PESTO

¾ cup loosely packed fresh basil leaves

2 tablespoons freshly grated Parmesan cheese

1 tablespoon extra-virgin olive oil

1 tablespoon chicken broth

1 tablespoon light sour cream

1 small garlic clove

Fresh basil sprigs, for garnish (optional)

# CURRIED LENTIL &
# AMARANTH SOUP WITH SPINACH

SMALL, ROUNDED FRENCH LENTILS WILL HOLD
THEIR SHAPE BETTER WHEN COOKED BUT BROWN LENTILS CAN
BE USED AS WELL. THE TINY AMARANTH GRAINS
(YOU COULD FIT AT LEAST TWO ON THE HEAD OF A PIN)
REMAIN CRUNCHY AFTER COOKING.

2 tablespoons olive oil

1 large onion, chopped

2 garlic cloves, minced

2 teaspoons cumin seeds

¾ teaspoon ground coriander

¾ teaspoon ground turmeric

½ teaspoon ground ginger

½ teaspoon freshly ground
   black pepper

4 cups chicken broth

1¼ cups French green lentils,
   picked over & rinsed

½ cup amaranth

1 pound boiling or baking
   potatoes, scrubbed &
   cut into ½-inch chunks

3 cups torn stemmed spinach

¼ teaspoon salt

Plain yogurt, for garnish

In a Dutch oven or heavy large saucepan, heat the oil over medium heat. Add the onion and garlic and sauté for 3 to 4 minutes, or until tender. In a cup, mix together the cumin, coriander, turmeric, ginger, and pepper. Add the spice mixture to the onion and sauté, stirring constantly, for 1 minute.

Add the broth, 2 cups water, the lentils, and amaranth to the pot. Bring to a boil over high heat. Reduce the heat to low, cover and simmer, stirring occasionally, for 30 minutes.

Stir in the potatoes, increase the heat to medium-low, and cover. Simmer for 15 to 20 minutes longer, or until the lentils and potatoes are tender. Stir in the spinach and salt and simmer, uncovered, for 5 minutes, or until the spinach is wilted but still bright green. Serve the soup in warmed bowls topped with a big spoonful of yogurt.

# SCOTCH BROTH WITH ROASTED GARLIC & WINTER VEGETABLES

THIS BRACING SOUP IS PERFECT FOR

A COLD WINTER DAY. CELERIAC, ALSO KNOWN AS

CELERY ROOT, HAS A MILD CELERY FLAVOR.

IF IT IS UNAVAILABLE, SUBSTITUTE REGULAR STALK

CELERY OR ADD PEELED JERUSALEM ARTICHOKES.

Preheat the oven to 450°F.

Place the lamb shanks in a 13- by 9-inch baking pan. Rinse one of the onions, leaving it unpeeled, and cut it into six equal wedges. Add the onion wedges and garlic to the baking pan. Roast the lamb shanks, onion, and garlic, turning the shanks 2 or 3 times, for about 30 minutes, or until the shanks, garlic, and onion are browned.

Discard the fat in the pan. Place the shanks, onion, and garlic in a large pot, add 6 cups water and bring to a boil over high heat, skimming off the foam that rises to the surface. Partially cover the pot, reduce the heat to low, and cook slowly, so the liquid is barely simmering, not boiling, for about 1¼ hours, or until the meat is fork-tender.

Meanwhile, peel and dice the remaining onion. In a heavy medium-size saucepan, heat the oil over medium heat. Stir in the diced onion, thyme, and pepper and cook, stirring frequently, for about 6 minutes, or until the onion is tender. Stir in the broth and barley. Increase the heat to high and bring to a boil. Reduce the heat to low, cover, and simmer for 30 to 35 minutes, or until the barley is tender but still firm. Remove the pot from the heat and set aside, covered. *(continued overleaf)*

3 lamb shanks, about 1 pound each, well trimmed

2 large onions

1 whole head garlic, halved crosswise

1 tablespoon olive oil

½ teaspoon dried thyme, crumbled

½ teaspoon freshly ground black pepper

3 cups chicken broth

⅓ cup pearled barley

1 bay leaf, preferably Turkish

2 large carrots, diced

1 small leek, halved, rinsed & cut lengthwise into strips

1 cup diced peeled celeriac

¾ cup diced peeled white turnip

¾ teaspoon salt

Remove the shanks and garlic from the pot and let stand until cool enough to handle. Cut the meat from the shanks and dice, discarding the fat, sinews, and the flat, grayish pieces of meat. Cover the meat loosely with foil to keep it moist. Squeeze the pulp from the papery skin of the garlic cloves into a small bowl and mash the pulp.

Pour the lamb broth through a fine-mesh sieve back into the cooking pot and skim off the fat. Add the barley mixture, carrots, leek, celeriac, turnip, and mashed garlic and bring to a boil over high heat. Reduce the heat to medium-low, cover, and simmer for 5 minutes, or until the vegetables are tender.

Stir in the meat and salt and simmer for 5 minutes longer, or until heated through.

# SWEET & SOUR BEET SOUP
# WITH WHEAT BERRIES

SERVES 8 TO 10

IF YOUR GRANDMOTHER WAS OF EASTERN EUROPEAN
DESCENT, SHE MIGHT HAVE MADE A SOUP LIKE THIS, WHICH IS REALLY A
HOT BORSCHT, FULL OF VEGETABLES WITH A ROBUST SWEET-
AND-SOUR FLAVOR. YOU CAN COOK THE WHEAT BERRIES AND BEETS
UP TO TWO DAYS AHEAD AND STORE IN THE REFRIGERATOR.

6 cups chicken broth

½ cup wheat berries, rinsed

1¼ pounds beets with greens
(about 3 beets)

2 tablespoons olive oil

1 large onion, chopped

2 large celery stalks, diced

1 large carrot, diced

3 tablespoons packed light
brown sugar

1 tablespoon grated peeled
fresh ginger

½ teaspoon dried thyme, crumbled

½ teaspoon freshly ground
black pepper

¼ teaspoon ground allspice

2 cups coarsely shredded (about
¼ inch wide) green cabbage

2 medium-size tart green apples,
cored & cut into ½-inch dice

2 tablespoons red wine vinegar

Sour cream & snipped fresh dill,
for garnish

In a heavy medium-size saucepan, bring 1 cup broth and 1 cup water to a boil over high heat. Stir in the wheat berries and return to a boil. Reduce the heat to low, cover, and simmer for 1½ to 2 hours, or until the wheat berries have swelled into a round shape and are tender but still firm. Drain, discarding the liquid, and set the wheat berries aside.

Meanwhile, trim off all but 1 inch of the beet tops and scrub the beets. Trim the stems from the leaves and cut the leaves into strips and set aside.

In a large saucepan, combine the beets with enough cold water to cover. Cover and bring to a boil over high heat. Reduce the heat to medium and simmer for about 40 minutes, or until the beets are fork-tender. Drain the beets in a colander and rinse briefly under cold running water. Let cool until warm. Slip off the skins, cut the beets into ½-inch dice, and set aside.

In a large, nonreactive Dutch oven, heat the oil over medium heat. Add the onion, celery, and carrot and cook, stirring frequently, for 6 to 8 minutes, or until the vegetables are tender. Stir in the sugar, ginger, thyme, pepper, and allspice and cook, stirring constantly for 30 seconds. Stir in the cabbage, apples, and beet greens. Reduce the heat to low, cover and cook, stirring several times, for 5 minutes, or until the vegetables are wilted.

Add the remaining 5 cups broth, 1 cup water, the diced beets, and the wheat berries to the pot. Increase the heat to high and bring to a boil. Reduce the heat to medium-low, cover, and simmer for 5 minutes, or until the flavors are blended and the soup is heated through.

Remove the pot from the heat and stir in the vinegar. Ladle into warmed soup bowls and top with sour cream and snipped dill.

# TABBOULEH WITH PRESERVED LEMONS IN ROMAINE LEAVES

SERVES 4 TO 6

MUCH BELOVED IN MOROCCAN COOKING, PRESERVED LEMONS
COUPLE WELL WITH THE MINT IN THIS STANDARD BULGUR SALAD, ADDING
A REFRESHING SALTY-SOUR NOTE. THE LEMONS HAVE BEEN
PICKLED IN A SPECIAL BRINE AND SHOULD BE RINSED BEFORE USE. IF YOU
WISH, YOU CAN OMIT THEM WITHOUT DETRIMENT TO THE SALAD.

Place the bulgur in a large bowl and add the boiling water and 2 tablespoons lemon juice; let stand for 30 minutes, or until the bulgur is softened and tender. Drain in a fine-mesh sieve, pressing down on the bulgur to remove any excess moisture. Dry the bowl and return the bulgur to the bowl.

Add the parsley, cucumber, tomatoes, green onions, mint, preserved lemon peel and pulp, the oil, salt, pepper, and the remaining 6 tablespoons lemon juice to the bulgur and toss to blend well.

Remove the large outer leaves from the romaine and save for another salad. Rinse the smaller inner leaves and dry.

To serve, either mound the tabbouleh in the center of a large platter and surround with the romaine leaves, letting guests fill their own leaves with the salad, or fill the leaves with the tabbouleh and arrange on a platter. Garnish with feta, sliced tomatoes and olives, if desired. Serve freshly made.

½ cup fine- or medium-grain bulgur wheat

1½ cups boiling water

½ cup fresh lemon juice

1½ cups minced fresh flat-leaf parsley

1 cup finely diced peeled seeded cucumber

1 cup finely diced plum tomatoes

¾ cup thinly sliced green onions

¾ cup minced fresh mint leaves

3 tablespoons minced rinsed preserved lemon peel

1 tablespoon minced preserved lemon pulp

2 tablespoons extra-virgin olive oil

¾ teaspoon salt

½ teaspoon freshly ground black pepper

2 or 3 large heads romaine lettuce

Feta cheese, tomato wedges & olives, for garnish (optional)

# MILLET & GREEN PEA SALAD WITH LEMON-DILL VINAIGRETTE

TOASTING THE MILLET ADDS A NUTTY
FLAVOR AND HELPS TO KEEP THE GRAINS SEPARATE
DURING COOKING, THOUGH THEY STILL
RETAIN A SLIGHTLY STICKY TEXTURE. DO NOT
RINSE THE MILLET BEFORE TOASTING.

½ cup millet

1 teaspoon olive oil

1¼ cups boiling water

⅛ teaspoon salt

1 cup frozen green peas

LEMON-DILL VINAIGRETTE

3 tablespoons olive oil

2 tablespoons fresh lemon juice

1 teaspoon Dijon mustard

¼ teaspoon salt

¼ teaspoon freshly ground
　black pepper

2 tablespoons snipped fresh dill

2 cups thinly shredded
　romaine lettuce

1 medium-size yellow bell pepper,
　cored, seeded & cut into
　thin strips

½ cup sliced green onions

In a heavy medium-size saucepan, stir together the millet and oil until well coated. Over medium-high heat, sauté the millet, stirring frequently, for 2 to 3 minutes, or until the grains smell toasty and start to crackle.

Pour the boiling water into the saucepan, add the salt, and return to a boil. Reduce the heat to low, cover, and simmer for 25 to 30 minutes, or until the grains are tender and have burst, and the liquid is absorbed. Remove the pan from the heat and stir in the peas. Transfer to a medium-size bowl, cover loosely with a sheet of waxed paper to keep it moist, and refrigerate for 20 to 30 minutes, or until cooled.

Meanwhile, prepare the vinaigrette: In a large salad bowl, whisk together the olive oil, lemon juice, Dijon mustard, salt, and pepper until well blended. Stir in the dill.

To serve, add the romaine, bell pepper, and green onions to the dressing and toss to combine. Add the millet and pea mixture and toss again.

# WHEAT BERRY & ORANGE SALAD WITH PROSCIUTTO & ARUGULA

SMOKED TURKEY AND CHICKEN ARE GOOD SUBSTITUTES
FOR THE PROSCIUTTO IN THIS SALAD. ADD A FEW
FRESH RASPBERRIES FOR GARNISH IF YOU LIKE, BUT ONLY
A FEW. THE WHEAT BERRIES MAY BE COOKED UP TO
TWO DAYS AHEAD AND REFRIGERATED.

In a heavy medium-size saucepan, bring 3 cups water to a boil over high heat. Stir in the wheat berries and ⅛ teaspoon each salt and pepper, and return to a boil. Reduce the heat to low, cover, and simmer gently for about 2 hours, or until the wheat berries are very tender but not mushy and have puffed into a round shape. Check them occasionally and add water if the mixture becomes too dry. Drain the wheat berries in a colander and let cool until warm.

Meanwhile, with a serrated knife, remove the peel and all the white pith from the orange. Working over a bowl, cut out the orange sections from in between the membrane, letting the juice drip into the bowl, and place the sections in a bowl. Squeeze the juice from the membrane into the bowl (you will need about 1 tablespoon juice).

In a large salad bowl, whisk together the oil, vinegar, orange juice, sugar, and the remaining ¼ teaspoon salt and ⅛ teaspoon pepper until well combined.

To serve, add the arugula to the dressing in the salad bowl and toss to coat. Add the warm wheat berries, prosciutto, green onions, and orange sections and toss again.

¾ cup wheat berries, rinsed

⅛ teaspoon plus ¼ teaspoon salt

¼ teaspoon freshly ground black pepper

1 medium-size navel orange

2 tablespoons extra-virgin olive oil

1 tablespoon plus 1 teaspoon raspberry vinegar

¼ teaspoon sugar

1 bunch arugula, tough stems removed

2 ounces sliced prosciutto (not paper-thin), without fat, cut into strips

¼ cup thinly sliced green onions

# MEDITERRANEAN COUSCOUS & CHICKEN SALAD

SERVES 4

The tanginess of the citrus dressing, accented with
toasted cumin, marries wonderfully with the couscous
and chicken in this refreshing summer salad.
Refrigerated, the salad tastes even better the next
day and makes a flavorful lunch.

⅔ cup couscous

⅓ cup slivered dried apricot halves

1 cup chicken broth

8 ounces boneless skinless
chicken breasts, cut into
½-inch chunks

CITRUS DRESSING

1½ teaspoons ground cumin

2 tablespoons extra-virgin olive oil

1 teaspoon grated orange zest

3 tablespoons fresh orange juice

2 tablespoons fresh lemon juice

¼ teaspoon sugar

¼ teaspoon salt

¼ teaspoon freshly ground
black pepper

1 medium-size red bell pepper,
cored, seeded & cut
into thin strips

¼ cup diced red onion

¼ cup chopped fresh
flat-leaf parsley

Lettuce leaves

Strips of lemon zest & red onion,
for garnish (optional)

In a medium-size saucepan, bring 1¼ cups water to a boil over high heat. Stir in the couscous and apricots. Cover, remove from the heat, and let stand for 5 minutes. Remove the lid and gently fluff the couscous without mashing the apricots. Cover loosely and let cool until warm.

In a medium-size skillet, bring the chicken broth to a boil high heat. Stir in the chicken, reduce the heat to medium-low and simmer, stirring frequently, for about 2 minutes, or until no longer pink in the center. Remove with a slotted spoon and cover to keep moist.

Return the chicken broth to high heat and boil rapidly for 5 to 7 minutes, or until reduced to about 2 tablespoons. Pour the reduced liquid through a fine-mesh sieve into a large salad bowl and set aside.

Prepare the dressing: In a small skillet, toast the cumin over medium heat, stirring frequently, for 2 to 3 minutes, or until fragrant. Immediately tip the cumin into the salad bowl. Whisk in the oil, orange zest and juice, lemon juice, sugar, salt, and pepper until well combined.

Add the chicken, the couscous and apricot mixture, bell pepper, diced red onion, and parsley to the dressing in the bowl and toss gently. Spoon the salad into lettuce leaves and garnish with lemon zest and red onion strips, if desired.

# SHRIMP & FENNEL SALAD WITH KAMUT

SERVES 4

KAMUT, A LARGE OVAL-SHAPED GRAIN,
ADDS A NUTTY, EARTHY FLAVOR TO THIS SALAD, WHICH
CONTRASTS WITH THE LIGHTER FLAVORS OF
THE SHRIMP AND FENNEL. IF YOU CAN'T FIND KAMUT,
USE WHEAT BERRIES OR SPELT.

1 cup kamut, rinsed

2 red bell peppers, cored, seeded & cut into large flat pieces

⅛ teaspoon salt plus ½ teaspoon

⅛ teaspoon hot pepper flakes

12 ounces medium-size shrimp in the shell, rinsed

2 tablespoons extra-virgin olive oil

1 tablespoon plus 1 teaspoon red wine vinegar

2 teaspoons balsamic vinegar

¼ teaspoon freshly ground black pepper

1½ cups thinly sliced fresh fennel bulb

½ small red onion, halved & thinly sliced crosswise

16 Calamata olives, pitted & sliced

In a heavy large saucepan, bring 4 cups of water to a boil and add the kamut. Reduce the heat to low, cover, and simmer for about 1 hour, or until the grains have swelled and are tender. Drain in a colander, and let cool until warm.

Meanwhile, preheat the broiler, with the pan 5 inches from the heat source. Place the bell pepper pieces, skin side up, on the broiler rack. Broil, without turning, for 10 to 12 minutes, or until the skin is charred and blistered. Place in a small bowl, cover with plastic wrap, and let stand until cool enough to handle. Peel off the skin and cut the peppers into ½-inch-wide strips.

Meanwhile, fill a large skillet with 1 inch of water. Add the ⅛ teaspoon salt and the hot pepper flakes and bring to a boil over high heat. Add the shrimp, reduce the heat to medium-low, and cook, stirring frequently, for 3 to 4 minutes, or until they are firm and pink. Drain and cool under cold running water. Peel, devein, and cut each shrimp in half lengthwise.

In a large salad bowl, whisk together the oil, vinegars, pepper, and the remaining ½ teaspoon salt. Add the roasted peppers, fennel, red onion, and olives and toss to mix. Let marinate for 20 minutes.

Add the kamut and shrimp and toss to combine.

# FRESH CORN & BARLEY SALAD WITH SOUR CREAM-CHIVE DRESSING

REMEMBER THIS SALAD DURING THOSE SUMMER
WEEKS WHEN CORN IS AT ITS PEAK — THEN JUST ADD THE
SWEET, TENDER KERNELS RAW. SERVED AT ROOM
TEMPERATURE OR CHILLED, THE SALAD IS DELICIOUS AS A LIGHT
LUNCH WITH SMOKED TROUT OR OTHER SMOKED FISH.

In a heavy medium-size saucepan, bring the broth and 1¼ cups water to a boil over high heat. Stir in the barley and return to a boil. Reduce the heat to low, cover, and simmer for 25 to 30 minutes, or until the barley is just tender but still slightly firm to the bite. If using fresh corn, stir in the corn. Increase the heat to medium, cover, and simmer 5 to 7 minutes longer, or until the corn is just tender. (Most of the cooking liquid will be absorbed.) Transfer the barley mixture to a large salad bowl. If using frozen corn, stir into the barley mixture and remove it from the heat. Let stand, covered, for 5 minutes, then transfer to the salad bowl. Let the mixture cool until warm, stirring occasionally.

Meanwhile, prepare the dressing: In a small bowl, whisk together the sour cream, vinegar, salt, and pepper until well blended. Stir in the snipped chives and shallots.

To serve, add the dressing, tomatoes, and cucumber to the barley mixture and stir to combine. Serve at room temperature or chilled, on endive, if desired.

1 cup chicken broth

½ cup pearl barley

2 cups fresh corn kernels (3 or 4 medium-size ears) or frozen kernels

SOUR CREAM & CHIVE DRESSING

¼ cup light sour cream

1 tablespoon plus 1 teaspoon red wine vinegar

½ teaspoon salt

⅛ teaspoon freshly ground black pepper

2 tablespoons snipped fresh chives

2 tablespoons minced shallots or red onion

1 medium-size tomato, halved & thinly sliced

½ medium-size cucumber, thinly sliced

Belgian endive leaves (optional)

*Fresh Corn & Barley Salad with
Sour Cream—Chive Dressing (overleaf)*

# KASHA-STUFFED CABBAGE WITH SWEET & SAVORY TOMATO SAUCE

SERVES 4

THIS IS A MEATLESS VERSION OF A CLASSIC DISH, YET
IT HAS ALL THE HEARTINESS OF THE TRADITIONAL PREPARATION.
COOK A FEW EXTRA CABBAGE LEAVES IN CASE
SOME TEAR. FOR A COMPLETELY VEGETARIAN DISH, REPLACE
THE BEEF BROTH WITH VEGETABLE BROTH.

2 tablespoons olive oil

2 large onions, diced

1 tablespoon sugar

½ teaspoon dried thyme, crumbled

½ teaspoon ground ginger

¼ teaspoon ground allspice

⅛ teaspoon cayenne

2 garlic cloves, minced

1¼ cups beef broth

3 large eggs

¾ cup medium-grain kasha

12 large to medium-size
    cabbage leaves

1 (16-ounce) can whole tomatoes
    in purée, tomatoes
    coarsely chopped

1 (14½-ounce) can stewed tomatoes

½ cup orange juice

1 tablespoon tomato paste

½ teaspoon salt

½ teaspoon freshly ground
    black pepper

3 tablespoons snipped fresh dill,
    plus additional for garnish

Sour cream (optional)

In a heavy large nonstick skillet, heat the oil over medium heat. Stir in the onions. Sprinkle with the sugar, thyme, ginger, allspice, and cayenne. Reduce the heat to medium-low and cook, stirring frequently, for about 25 minutes, or until the onions are very tender and light golden. Stir in the garlic and cook for 30 seconds, or until fragrant. Transfer to a bowl, cover, and set aside. Wash and dry the skillet.

In a small saucepan, bring the beef broth and ¼ cup water to a boil over high heat.

Beat 1 egg in a small bowl. Stir in the kasha. Heat the skillet over medium heat until it feels warm when you hold your hand above it. Add the kasha mixture to the skillet and cook, stirring constantly and scraping the bottom of the pan, for 2 to 4 minutes, or until the grains are dry and separate and smell toasted. Stir in half the onions and the broth and return to a boil. Reduce the heat to low, cover, and simmer for 25 minutes, or until the kasha is tender and the liquid nearly absorbed. Transfer to a bowl and let cool.

Meanwhile, bring a large pot of salted water to a boil over high heat. Add the cabbage leaves 2 or 3 at a time, press them down into the water with a wooden spoon and cook, uncovered, 2 to 3 minutes, or until pliable. Remove with tongs to a colander; cool under cold running water, and place

between paper towels to drain well. Repeat with the remaining leaves.

Place the remaining onions in a heavy large nonreactive saucepan. Stir in the tomatoes with the purée, the stewed tomatoes, orange juice, and tomato paste and bring to a boil over medium-high heat. Reduce the heat to medium-low and simmer, stirring frequently, for 15 minutes, or until the flavors are blended and the sauce is thickened. Stir in ¼ teaspoon salt and ¼ teaspoon pepper. Remove the saucepan from the heat. *(continued overleaf)*

*(Kasha-Stuffed Cabbage continued)*

Preheat the oven to 375°F. Spread 1½ cups sauce in a 13- by 9- by 2-inch baking dish.

Add the remaining eggs, 3 tablespoons dill, and the remaining salt and pepper to the cooled kasha and mix well.

To roll the cabbage, pare the thick part of the core from the bottom of a cabbage leaf and trim the end. Spoon a scant ¼ cup kasha filling on the lower half of the leaf and shape the filling into a thick sausage. Fold the end of the leaf over the filling, fold over the sides, and roll up. Place, seam side down, in the sauce in the prepared baking dish. Repeat with the remaining leaves and filling.

Spoon the remaining sauce over the cabbage rolls and cover with foil. Bake for 20 minutes. Uncover and bake for 20 minutes longer, or until the sauce is thick and bubbly. Sprinkle the cabbage with the remaining 2 tablespoons dill and serve with the sauce, sour cream, and snipped dill, if desired.

# GREENS & POSOLE
# WITH LIME & CILANTRO

SERVES 4

*POSOLE* IS ANOTHER NAME FOR WHOLE HOMINY AS
WELL AS THE NAME OF THIS STEW, AND IT IS LOVELY SERVED
WITH CORN BREAD OR AS A SIDE DISH WITH
ROAST PORK. POSOLE IS AVAILABLE IN CANS, BUT IF YOU
PREFER TO USE DRIED FOLLOW THE NOTE BELOW.

3 tablespoons olive oil

2 cups chopped white onions

3 large garlic cloves, minced

1 large jalapeño, cored & minced,
   with some of the seeds

1 ½ teaspoons ground coriander

½ teaspoon salt

½ teaspoon freshly ground
   black pepper

5 cups packed torn
   & stemmed kale

5 cups cut Swiss chard (stems
   in 1-inch pieces & leaves
   in 2-inch pieces)

5 cups packed torn
   & stemmed spinach

1 ¼ cups chicken broth

1 (16-ounce) can whole hominy,
   drained & rinsed

½ cup chopped fresh cilantro leaves
   with some of the stems

2 to 3 tablespoons fresh lime juice

Chopped white onion, for garnish

In a Dutch oven, heat the oil over medium-high heat. Add the onions, garlic, jalapeño pepper, coriander, salt, and pepper and cook, stirring frequently, for 4 to 5 minutes, or until the onions start to become tender.

A handful at a time, stir in the greens, first the kale, then the chard, and then the spinach, adding a little of the broth with each addition, as necessary as the pot gets dry.

When all the greens have been added, stir in the remaining broth and the hominy. Increase the heat to high and bring to a boil. Reduce the heat to medium-low, cover, and simmer for 10 minutes, or until the flavors are blended, the greens are tender, and the hominy is heated through. Remove from the heat and stir in the cilantro and lime juice, to taste. Ladle into warmed bowls, sprinkle each with a little raw onion, and serve.

NOTE:

If you prefer to cook dried whole hominy, soak ½ cup in water to cover overnight. Drain in a colander, put in a saucepan and add fresh water to cover by 2 inches. Bring to a boil and simmer, covered, over low heat, for 1 ½ to 2 hours, or until tender.

# MEDITERRANEAN VEGETABLES
## WITH QUINOA

SERVES 4

THE SLIGHTLY CRUNCHY QUALITY OF THE QUINOA IS A
PERFECT FOIL TO THE TENDER VEGETABLES IN THIS HEARTY STEW.
SAUTÉING VEGETABLES IN CHICKEN BROTH AND A BIT OF OIL
IS A HANDY, LOW-FAT COOKING TECHNIQUE. A TOPPING OF CHOPPED
PARSLEY OR FRESH BASIL MAKES THE FLAVORS SPARKLE.

In a nonreactive Dutch oven, heat the oil over medium heat. Stir in the onion, garlic, basil, thyme, fennel seeds, and hot pepper flakes and cook, stirring frequently, for 2 to 3 minutes, or until the onion begins to soften.

Add the eggplant and cook, stirring frequently, and drizzling with ½ cup of the ⅔ cup broth, about 2 tablespoons at a time, for 10 to 15 minutes, or until the eggplant is tender. Stir in the bell peppers and drizzle with the remainder of the ⅔ cup broth, reduce the heat to medium-low, cover, and cook for 5 to 6 minutes, or until crisp-tender.

Uncover the pot and add the squashes, tossing to mix. Stir in the tomatoes. Increase the heat to medium and bring to a simmer. Cover and cook, stirring frequently, for 12 to 15 minutes, or until the vegetables are tender. Season with the salt and ¼ teaspoon pepper.

Meanwhile, in a heavy medium-size saucepan, bring the 2 cups broth to a boil over high heat. Stir in the quinoa and the remaining ¼ teaspoon pepper and return to a boil. Reduce the heat to low, cover, and simmer for 20 minutes, or until the quinoa is translucent and the liquid is absorbed.

Transfer the quinoa to a platter. Spoon the vegetable mixture in the center and serve.

3 tablespoons extra-virgin olive oil

1 medium-size onion, chopped

5 garlic cloves, minced

½ teaspoon dried basil, crumbled

¼ teaspoon dried thyme, crumbled

¼ teaspoon fennel seeds

⅛ teaspoon hot pepper flakes

1 medium-size eggplant, cut into 1-inch cubes

⅔ cup chicken broth plus 2 cups

1 medium-size red bell pepper, cored, seeded & cut into ½-inch chunks

1 medium-size yellow bell pepper, cored, seeded & cut into ½-inch chunks

1 medium-size zucchini, halved lengthwise & cut crosswise into ¼-inch slices

1 medium-size yellow summer squash, halved lengthwise & cut crosswise into ¼-inch slices

1 (28-ounce) can plum tomatoes in juice, well drained & coarsely chopped

½ teaspoon salt

½ teaspoon freshly ground black pepper

1 cup quinoa, rinsed for 2 minutes

# TAMALE PIE WITH CHEDDAR & CORNMEAL CRUST

SERVES 8

THIS HEARTY PIE WITH ITS SPICY MEAT AND
BEAN FILLING AND CORNMEAL CRUST (ELEMENTS BORROWED
FROM THE WELL-KNOWN MEXICAN TAMALE)
IS PERFECT POTLUCK FARE—IT'S EVEN BETTER WHEN
REHEATED. SERVE WITH A GREEN SALAD.

## FILLING

4 teaspoons olive oil

1 medium-size green bell pepper, cored, seeded & diced

1 medium-size red bell pepper, cored, seeded & diced

1 medium-size onion, chopped

8 ounces lean ground beef

2½ teaspoons ground cumin

¾ teaspoon ground coriander

½ teaspoon dried oregano

½ teaspoon black pepper

1 (19-ounce) can red kidney beans, rinsed and drained

1 (16-ounce) can crushed tomatoes

½ cup medium-hot salsa

½ cup sliced pimiento-stuffed green olives

## CRUST

1½ cups yellow cornmeal

1 cup all-purpose flour

1 teaspoon baking powder

½ teaspoon baking soda

¼ teaspoon salt

1¼ cups plain low-fat yogurt

2 large eggs

2 tablespoons olive oil

1 cup shredded sharp cheddar cheese

½ cup chopped green onions

Preheat the oven to 375°F. Grease a 13- by 9- by 2-inch baking dish.

Prepare the filling: In a heavy large nonstick skillet, heat the oil over medium-high heat. Add the green and red bell peppers and onion and sauté for 6 to 8 minutes, or until the vegetables begin to soften. Crumble in the beef; toss to mix. Increase the heat to high and sauté, breaking apart clumps of meat, for 3 minutes, until the meat is no longer pink.

Stir in the cumin, coriander, oregano, and pepper and sauté, stirring constantly, for 30 seconds. Add the beans, tomatoes, salsa, olives, and ¼ cup water and bring to a boil. Remove from the heat and pour the filling into the prepared baking dish.

Prepare the crust: In a large bowl, combine the cornmeal, flour, baking powder, baking soda, and salt, stirring until well mixed.

In a bowl, whisk together the yogurt, eggs, and oil until well blended. Stir in ¾ cup cheddar and the green onions. Pour the yogurt mixture over the cornmeal mixture and stir just until blended. Spoon dollops of the mixture over the filling and spread evenly. Sprinkle with the remaining ¼ cup cheddar.

Bake for 25 to 30 minutes, or until the filling is bubbly and the crust is lightly browned and firm. Cool on a rack for a few minutes before serving.

# BEEF & BARLEY STEW WITH BUTTERNUT SQUASH & APRICOTS

BE SURE TO USE TART CALIFORNIA DRIED APRICOTS,
RATHER THAN THE SWEETER TURKISH VARIETY. THIS STEW TASTES
EVEN BETTER THE NEXT DAY SINCE THE FLAVORS
BLEND TOGETHER AND INTENSIFY. SERVE IT WITH HOT BISCUITS
FOR A WARMING FALL OR WINTER MEAL.

Season the beef with ¼ teaspoon each salt and pepper. Toss with 1 tablespoon of flour to coat.

In a Dutch oven or heavy large saucepan, heat 2 tablespoons of the oil over medium-high heat. Add the beef and cook, turning often, for 3 to 4 minutes, or until browned. Add the onion and garlic and sauté for 2 to 3 minutes, or until nearly tender.

Add the remaining 1 tablespoon oil to the pot and stir in the coriander, ginger, thyme, and the remaining ¼ teaspoon pepper; sauté for 30 seconds, stirring constantly. Sprinkle with the remaining flour and cook, stirring constantly, for 30 seconds. Add 2 cups of the broth and the wine and bring to a boil. Cover and simmer over low heat for 45 minutes, or until the meat is tender.

Meanwhile, in a medium-size saucepan, bring 1 cup water and the remaining broth to a boil over high heat. Stir in the barley, cover, and simmer over low heat for 30 minutes, or until tender. Drain well.

Stir the squash and apricots into the stew. Increase the heat to high and bring to a boil. Reduce the heat to low, cover, and simmer for 15 minutes, or until the squash is fork-tender. Stir in the barley and the remaining ¼ teaspoon salt. Increase the heat to medium-low and simmer, uncovered and stirring frequently, for 10 minutes, or until the stew is thickened.

12 ounces boneless beef chuck, well trimmed & cut into 1-inch cubes

½ teaspoon salt

½ teaspoon freshly ground black pepper

3 tablespoons all-purpose flour

3 tablespoons extra-virgin olive oil

1 cup coarsely chopped onion

2 garlic cloves, minced

¾ teaspoon ground coriander

½ teaspoon ground ginger

½ teaspoon dried thyme, crumbled

2½ cups beef broth

⅔ cup dry red wine

⅓ cup pearl barley

2 cups 1-inch chunks peeled butternut squash

1 cup dried apricots, halved

# SAUTÉED KIBBEE WITH CURRANTS & SPICED YOGURT SAUCE

SERVES 4

ACCORDING TO PAULA WOLFERT, *KIBBEE,* IN ITS MOST CLASSIC
FORM, IS FINELY GROUND LAMB KNEADED WITH FINE-GRAINED BULGUR
AND FORMED INTO SHELLS WHICH ARE STUFFED WITH A MEAT
MIXTURE. THE FOLLOWING RECIPE IS A STREAMLINED VERSION—THE
MEAT IS SHAPED INTO PATTIES, WITHOUT A FILLING, AND BROILED.

SPICE MIXTURE

¾ teaspoon salt

½ teaspoon freshly ground
    black pepper

½ teaspoon ground ginger

¼ teaspoon ground allspice

⅛ teaspoon ground cardamom

⅛ teaspoon ground cinnamon

⅛ teaspoon cayenne, or to taste

MEAT MIXTURE & SAUCE

⅓ cup fine-grain bulgur

12 ounces lean ground
    lamb or beef

¼ cup finely minced onion

¼ cup minced fresh flat-leaf parsley

2 tablespoons dried currants

2 tablespoons fresh lemon juice

½ cup plain low-fat yogurt

2 tablespoons diced red bell pepper

2 tablespoons diced
    peeled cucumber

About 2 teaspoons extra-virgin
    olive oil

Prepare the spice mixture: In a cup, mix together all the ingredients.

Prepare the meat mixture: In a small bowl, combine the bulgur and ½ cup warm water and let stand for 15 minutes. Drain through a fine-mesh sieve, squeezing the moisture from the bulgur. In a large bowl, combine the bulgur, lamb, onion, 3 tablespoons parsley, the currants, 1 tablespoon lemon juice, and 2 teaspoons spice mixture. With your hands, work the meat mixture thoroughly, squeezing it thorough your fingers and pressing it with your knuckles, for about 4 minutes, or until well blended. Cover and refrigerate for 30 minutes.

Meanwhile, in a small bowl, mix the yogurt, bell pepper, cucumber, remaining spice mixture and parsley and 1 tablespoon lemon juice. Cover and refrigerate the sauce.

Preheat the broiler with the pan 4 to 5 inches from the heat source. Brush the hot broiler pan lightly with oil.

Form the meat mixture into 12 equal, oval-shaped patties, using about 2½ tablespoons for each. Place on the prepared rack and brush lightly with the olive oil.

Broil, without turning, for 5 to 6 minutes, or until lightly browned and just cooked through but still moist. Serve with the yogurt sauce.

# SPICY CORNMEAL-COATED CATFISH
# WITH CILANTRO SALSA

OVEN-FRYING THE CATFISH, INSTEAD OF PAN-FRYING IT,
GREATLY REDUCES THE FAT NORMALLY FOUND IN THIS DISH.
SERVE WITH SLICED FRESH TOMATOES OR COLESLAW
AND LIME WEDGES TO SQUEEZE OVER THE FISH. LOOK FOR
FIRM CATFISH THAT HAS A LIGHT PINK COLOR.

Coat two jelly-roll pans with 1 tablespoon oil each. Cut the catfish fillets in half along the center. Cut thick pieces of catfish into 2-inch lengths, thinner pieces into 3-inch lengths.

In a cup, mix together the cumin, salt, pepper, and cayenne. In a medium-size bowl, combine the catfish, 1½ teaspoons seasoning mix, and the lime juice and toss to coat the fish. In a shallow bowl, beat the eggs. In a pie plate, combine the cornmeal, flour, and the remaining seasoning mix and stir until well mixed.

One at a time, dip each piece of fish into the eggs, letting the excess drip off, and then roll in the seasoned cornmeal, coating both sides and the ends. Place in a single layer on the prepared jelly-roll pans and let the fish stand while preparing the salsa.

Preheat the oven to 450°F.

Prepare the salsa: In a small bowl, stir together the cilantro, onion, bell pepper, lime juice, 1 tablespoon oil, jalapeño, cumin, and salt and stir to mix thoroughly.

Drizzle the fish with the 2 tablespoons oil. Bake for 6 to 8 minutes, or until browned on the underside. Turn the fish over and bake for 4 to 6 minutes longer, or until the crumbs are crisp and lightly browned and the fish is opaque in the thickest part. Serve immediately with the salsa.

2 tablespoons olive oil

1½ pounds catfish fillets

1 teaspoon ground cumin

¾ teaspoon salt

½ teaspoon freshly ground
    black pepper

⅛ teaspoon cayenne

2 tablespoons fresh lime juice

2 large eggs

1 cup yellow cornmeal

½ cup all-purpose flour

CILANTRO SALSA

¾ cup chopped fresh cilantro,
    including some stems

¼ cup minced red onion

¼ cup minced red bell pepper

3 tablespoons fresh lime juice

1 tablespoon olive oil

2 teaspoons minced fresh
    jalapeño, with some
    of the seeds

¼ teaspoon ground cumin

¼ teaspoon salt

2 tablespoons olive oil

*Spicy Cornmeal-Coated Catfish*
*with Cilantro Salsa (overleaf)*

# LEMONY ROAST CHICKEN WITH MIDDLE-EASTERN BULGUR STUFFING

SERVES 6

THE MINT AND SUN-DRIED TOMATOES ARE
DELICIOUS ACCENTS IN THIS STUFFING. IF YOU DECIDE NOT
TO MAKE THE GRAVY, ADD A LITTLE MORE SALT
TO THE STUFFING AND DON'T ADD THE CHICKEN BROTH
TO THE PAN WHEN ROASTING THE CHICKEN.

MIDDLE-EASTERN STUFFING

1 cup medium-grain bulgur

3 cups boiling water

2 tablespoons unsalted butter

½ cup thinly sliced green onions

1 garlic clove, minced

1 teaspoon dried mint, crumbled

¼ cup chopped sun-dried tomatoes,
    packed in oil, drained &
    well blotted

¼ cup minced fresh
    flat-leaf parsley

¼ cup chicken broth

1 large egg

½ teaspoon salt

½ teaspoon freshly ground
    black pepper

LEMONY CHICKEN

1 (5½ to 6 pound)
    roasting chicken

¼ cup fresh lemon juice

½ teaspoon salt

½ teaspoon freshly ground
    black pepper

1½ teaspoons dried mint, crumbled

½ cup chicken broth

Prepare the stuffing: In a medium-size bowl, combine the bulgur and boiling water. Let stand for 30 minutes, or until much of the water is absorbed and the bulgur is tender. Pour through a fine-mesh sieve, pressing down to squeeze out the moisture. Return the bulgur to the bowl.

In a small skillet, melt the butter over medium heat. Add the green onions, garlic, and mint and cook, stirring frequently, for about 2 minutes, or until the onion is wilted. Add the green onion mixture, the sun-dried tomatoes, parsley, broth, egg, salt, and pepper to the bulgur and mix until well blended.

Preheat the oven to 350°F. Grease a 13- by 9-inch roasting pan and a small baking pan.

Prepare the chicken: Rinse it inside and out, and pat dry with paper towels. Rub the cavity with 1 tablespoon lemon juice and ¼ teaspoon each salt and pepper. Loosely stuff the chicken, setting the extra aside. Secure the cavity with metal skewers. Place the chicken in the prepared roasting pan.

Rub the chicken skin with the remaining 3 tablespoons lemon juice. Sprinkle with the mint and the remaining ¼ teaspoon each salt and pepper. Pour the broth into the roasting pan. Spoon the remaining stuffing into the prepared baking pan, cover with foil, and refrigerate.

Roast the chicken, basting occasionally with the pan juices, for 1¾ to 2¼ hours, or until the skin is browned and crisp and the meat is no longer pink near the bone. Add a little chicken broth or water to the roasting pan if it gets dry; be sure there is always a little liquid in the pan. About 30 minutes before the chicken is done, place the pan of extra stuffing in the oven and bake until heated through. Transfer the chicken to a platter.

Prepare the gravy: Skim the fat from the pan juices. With a wooden spoon, scrape up any browned bits from the bottom of the pan. Pour the juices through a fine-mesh sieve into a medium-size saucepan. Stir in the broth and bring to a boil over high heat, skimming off the foam that rises to the surface. Reduce the heat to medium and simmer for 5 minutes. Pour any juices that have collected on the platter into the saucepan.

In a cup, dissolve the cornstarch in the lemon juice. Stir the cornstarch mixture into the saucepan and return to a boil. Cook, stirring constantly, for about 1 minute, or until thickened. Stir in the butter until melted. Remove the saucepan from the heat and season with salt and pepper, if desired.

Carve the chicken and serve with the stuffing and the pan gravy.

PAN GRAVY

1 cup chicken broth

1 tablespoon cornstarch

1 tablespoon fresh lemon juice

1 tablespoon unsalted butter

Salt & freshly ground black pepper, to taste

# BARLEY & WILD MUSHROOM PILAF

SERVES 4 TO 6

PILAFS ARE NOT ALWAYS MADE WITH RICE, AS THE
RECIPES ON THESE TWO PAGES SHOW. MIXED FRESH MUSHROOMS,
INCLUDING BUTTON, SHIITAKE, AND CREMINI, COMBINED
WITH DRIED MUSHROOMS, LEND A WOODSY FLAVOR TO THIS DISH.
ALWAYS REMOVE THE STEMS FROM SHIITAKE MUSHROOMS.

¼ cup mixed dried mushrooms, crumbled into large pieces

1 cup boiling water

2 tablespoons unsalted butter

1 medium-size onion, halved & thinly sliced

1 garlic clove, minced

¼ teaspoon dried thyme, crumbled

¼ teaspoon freshly ground black pepper

8 ounces mixed fresh mushrooms, sliced

¼ teaspoon salt

¾ cup pearl barley

2 cups boiling chicken broth

2 tablespoons chopped fresh flat-leaf parsley, for garnish

In a small bowl, combine the dried mushrooms and boiling water. Let stand for 10 to 15 minutes, or until softened. With a slotted spoon, lift the mushrooms from the soaking liquid to another bowl. Pour the soaking liquid through a fine-mesh sieve lined with cheesecloth into a measuring cup, leaving any grit behind.

In a heavy medium-size saucepan, melt the butter over medium-high heat. Add the onion, garlic, thyme, and pepper and cook, stirring occasionally, for 4 to 5 minutes, or until the onion is tender and starts to brown.

Stir in the fresh mushrooms. Sprinkle with the salt and 2 tablespoons of the mushroom soaking liquid and cook, stirring occasionally, for 4 to 5 minutes, or until the mushrooms are tender and the liquid is reduced. Stir in the barley, dried mushrooms, boiling broth, and the remaining mushroom soaking liquid. Bring to a boil. Reduce the heat to low, cover, and simmer for 30 to 35 minutes, or until the barley is tender and most of the liquid is absorbed. Let stand, covered, for 5 minutes. Sprinkle with the parsley and serve.

# WINTER VEGETABLE PILAF

THIS IS A WONDERFUL WINTER SIDE DISH TO
SERVE WITH GRILLED SALMON OR ROAST CHICKEN. THE BROWN,
OVAL GRAINS OF SPELT HAVE A DISTINCT NUTTY FLAVOR
AND THE VEGETABLES HAVE A NATURAL SWEETNESS. YOU MAY
COOK THE SPELT UP TO 2 DAYS AHEAD.

In a heavy medium-size saucepan, bring 1 cup of the broth and 2 cups water to a boil over high heat. Add the spelt and return to a boil. Reduce the heat to low, cover, and simmer for about 2 hours, or until the spelt has swelled and is tender but still has some bite. Drain, return to the saucepan, and cover to keep warm.

In a heavy large deep skillet, melt the butter over medium heat. Add the carrots, parsnip, leek, onion, and salt, tossing to mix. Drizzle with the remaining 2 tablespoons broth. Reduce the heat to medium-low, cover, and cook, stirring occasionally, for 8 to 10 minutes, or until the vegetables are very tender but not mushy.

Add the spelt to the vegetables. Season with pepper and toss with two spoons to mix.

1 cup plus 2 tablespoons chicken broth

¾ cup spelt, rinsed

2 tablespoons unsalted butter

2 to 3 large carrots, cut into julienne strips

1 large parsnip, peeled & cut into julienne strips

1 medium-size leek, halved lengthwise, rinsed & cut into julienne strips

1 medium-size onion, halved through root & cut lengthwise into thin slices

¼ teaspoon salt

½ teaspoon freshly ground black pepper

# KALE & SUN-DRIED TOMATO SPOON BREAD

SERVES 8

ALTHOUGH TRADITIONALLY A SIDE DISH TO SOP UP
CHICKEN GRAVY, THIS SPOON BREAD HAS ENOUGH HEARTY FLAVOR TO BE
SERVED ON ITS OWN AS A FIRST COURSE OR A LIGHT VEGETARIAN
LUNCH DISH, WITH A SALAD. THIS RECIPE IS BASED ON SARAH BELK'S
SPOON BREAD FROM HER BOOK, *AROUND THE SOUTHERN TABLE*.

2 tablespoons freshly grated
Parmesan cheese

3 tablespoons unsalted butter

1 garlic clove, minced

1½ cups finely chopped kale, thick
center stems removed

¼ cup minced sun-dried tomatoes,
packed in oil, drained &
well blotted

¾ teaspoon salt

¼ teaspoon freshly ground
black pepper

1 cup white or yellow cornmeal

1 cup milk

3 large eggs, separated, plus
1 large egg white

½ teaspoon sugar

½ teaspoon baking powder

Preheat the oven to 400°F. Generously butter a 2-quart soufflé dish; dust with the Parmesan.

In a medium-size nonstick skillet, melt 1 tablespoon butter over medium heat. Stir in the garlic and cook for about 30 seconds, or until fragrant. Stir in the kale, reduce the heat to medium-low, and cook, stirring frequently, for 6 to 7 minutes, or until the kale is bright green and very tender. Stir in the sun-dried tomatoes and set aside.

In a heavy large saucepan, combine 2 cups water, the salt, pepper, and remaining 2 tablespoons butter. Bring to a boil over high heat. Add the cornmeal in a slow, steady stream, whisking constantly. When all the cornmeal has been added, remove the pan from the heat. Whisk in the milk, then the egg yolks, one at a time, until well blended. Stir in the sugar and the baking powder.

In a large bowl, with an electric mixer at high speed, beat the 4 egg whites with a pinch of salt until stiff but not dry peaks form.

Stir the kale mixture into the cornmeal mixture. Stir in a spoonful of the egg whites to lighten; with a rubber spatula, fold in the remaining whites just until incorporated. Scrape the mixture into the prepared soufflé dish. Bake for 30 to 35 minutes, or until the top is puffed and browned and the edges shrink from the sides. Serve immediately.

# CREAMY POLENTA WIT
# GORGONZOLA & CHIVES

SERVES 4 TO 6

IN NORTHERN ITALY, POLENTA, NOT PASTA, IS A
STAPLE. IT CAN BE FRIED, BAKED, OR SERVED SOFT AND CREAMY
AS IT IS HERE. THE CHEESE SHOULD BE SWEET AND
MILD-FLAVORED; EITHER AN ITALIAN GORGONZOLA *DOLCE* OR
A WISCONSIN-PRODUCED GORGONZOLA.

In a heavy medium-size saucepan, bring 3 cups water and the salt to a boil over high heat. Add the cornmeal in a slow, steady stream, whisking constantly. Reduce the heat to medium-low and cook, stirring frequently and vigorously with a wooden spoon, being sure to scrape the sides of the pan for even cooking, for about 15 minutes, or until the polenta is very thick and smooth.

Remove the pan from the heat and stir in the milk and cream until well blended. Add the Gorgonzola, pepper, and nutmeg and beat with a spoon until the Gorgonzola is melted and creamy.

To serve, sprinkle the hot polenta with the chives and additional fresh pepper, if desired.

½ teaspoon salt

1 cup coarse-ground or regular yellow cornmeal

¾ cup milk

⅓ cup heavy cream

3 ounces Gorgonzola cheese, rind removed & cheese cut up

¼ teaspoon freshly ground black pepper

Pinch freshly grated nutmeg

2 tablespoons snipped fresh chives

# BAKED POLENTA WITH ASPARAGUS, TOMATOES & PARMESAN

SERVES 6

THE ACIDITY OF THE TOMATOES ACTS AS
A COUNTERBALANCE TO THIS CREAMY, DELICATE POLENTA.
SERVE ALONGSIDE A JUICY ROAST CHICKEN OR
HERBED LEG OF LAMB, OR LET IT BE THE STARRING ATTRACTION
AT A VEGETARIAN DINNER FOR FOUR.

½ teaspoon plus ⅛ teaspoon salt

1 cup coarse-ground or
   regular yellow cornmeal

2 tablespoons unsalted butter, cut
   into small pieces

½ cup coarsely grated fresh
   Parmesan cheese

1 pound asparagus, tough ends
   trimmed, cut into 2-inch
   diagonal pieces

2 ripe plum tomatoes, diced

⅛ teaspoon freshly ground
   black pepper

In a heavy large saucepan, combine 3¼ cups water and the ½ teaspoon salt. Bring to a boil over high heat. Add the cornmeal in a slow, steady stream, whisking constantly. Reduce the heat to medium-low and cook, stirring frequently with a wooden spoon, for 15 minutes, or until very thick.

Generously oil an 8½- by 4½-inch loaf pan and pour the polenta into the pan. Smooth the surface with a spatula. Cover and chill for at least 4 hours or overnight, until very cold and firm.

Turn the polenta out onto a cutting board, and cut into ½-inch-thick slices.

Preheat the oven to 450°F. Generously butter a 9-inch-square baking dish. Arrange the polenta in two overlapping rows in the prepared dish. Dot with the butter and sprinkle with ¼ cup of the Parmesan. Bake for about 20 minutes, or until very hot and lightly browned in spots.

Fill a large skillet with ½ inch of water and bring to a boil. Add the asparagus and cook for 2 minutes, until crisp-tender. Drain; cool with cold water.

Remove the polenta from the oven and scatter the asparagus and tomatoes on top. Season the vegetables with the remaining salt and the pepper and sprinkle with the remaining Parmesan cheese.

Bake for 5 to 8 minutes longer, or until bubbly. Let stand for 5 minutes before serving.

# CHEDDAR CHEESE GRITS
# WITH GREEN ONIONS & GARLIC

OLD-FASHIONED GRITS, SO LABELED ON THE PACKAGE,
REQUIRE LONGER COOKING AND ARE MORE TEXTURED THAN
THE INSTANT VARIETY. THIS CASSEROLE IS COMMONLY
PAIRED WITH *GRILLADES*, A STEW MADE WITH SCALLOPS OF VEAL
OR BEEF SIMMERED IN A RICH GRAVY.

½ teaspoon salt

¾ cup old-fashioned grits

2 tablespoons unsalted butter

½ cup thinly sliced green onions

1 small garlic clove, minced

1 large egg

½ teaspoon freshly ground
  black pepper

¼ teaspoon hot pepper sauce

1½ cups shredded sharp white
  cheddar cheese

2 tablespoons freshly grated
  Parmesan cheese

Preheat the oven to 350°F. Generously butter an 8- or 9-inch-square baking dish.

In a heavy medium-size saucepan, bring 3½ cups water and the salt to a boil over high heat. Add the grits in a slow, steady stream, whisking constantly. Reduce the heat to low, cover, and cook, stirring frequently with a wooden spoon, for 25 minutes, or until the grits are thickened and softened. Remove the pan from the heat and set aside, partially covered, for 5 minutes.

Meanwhile, in a small nonstick skillet, melt the butter over medium heat. Stir in the green onions and garlic and sauté about 1 minute, or until the green onions are wilted.

Stir the grits well to cool slightly and eliminate any lumps. Stir in the sautéed green onion mixture. Beat in the egg, pepper, and hot pepper sauce. Add 1¼ cups of the cheddar and the Parmesan and stir until melted and smooth. Pour the grits into the prepared baking dish and sprinkle with the remaining ¼ cup cheddar. Bake for about 20 minutes, or until the grits are very hot and the edges are bubbly and beginning to puff.

To serve, cool slightly, then cut into squares.

# KASHA VARNISHKES WITH ONION CONFIT

SERVES 6

KASHA *VARNISHKES*, BUCKWHEAT GROATS TOSSED WITH
BOW-TIE PASTA, IS JEWISH SOUL FOOD. THE CONFIT, SLICED ONIONS
AND A TOUCH OF SUGAR SLOWLY COOKED TO A DEEP
GOLDEN BROWN COLOR AND SWEET FLAVOR, TRANSFORMS THESE
SIMPLE INGREDIENTS INTO SOMETHING EXTRAORDINARY.

In a heavy medium-size nonstick skillet, heat 1 tablespoon butter and the oil over medium heat. Add the onions, sprinkle with the sugar and ¼ teaspoon salt, and toss to mix. Cook the onions slowly, stirring occasionally, and reducing the heat as they begin to brown, for 35 to 40 minutes, or until the onions are golden and very tender.

Meanwhile, in a medium-size bowl, beat the egg until well broken up. Stir in the kasha.

Heat a heavy 10-inch skillet over medium heat until it feels hot when you hold your hand above it. Add the kasha mixture and cook, stirring constantly and scraping the bottom of the pan, for 2 to 4 minutes, or until the grains are dry and separate and smell toasted. Pour in the boiling broth, add the remaining 1 tablespoon butter and ¼ teaspoon salt, and return to a boil. Reduce the heat to low, cover, and simmer for 25 to 30 minutes, or until the kasha is tender and most of the liquid is absorbed. Cover and set aside.

Meanwhile, in a medium-size saucepan of lightly salted boiling water, cook the bow-tie pasta, stirring frequently, for 6 to 8 minutes, or until the pasta is al dente, firm but tender. Drain.

In a warmed serving bowl, combine the kasha, pasta, onion confit, and pepper and toss to mix. Sprinkle with the chives and serve.

2 tablespoons unsalted butter

1 tablespoon olive oil

3 medium-size onions, halved & thinly sliced crosswise

1 teaspoon sugar

½ teaspoon salt

1 large egg

1 cup kasha

2 cups boiling chicken broth

¾ cup small bow-tie pasta

½ teaspoon freshly ground black pepper

3 tablespoons snipped fresh chives

# SPICED CORNMEAL & PUMPKIN LOAF

MAKES 1 LOAF

SERVE THIS FRAGRANT NOT-TOO-SWEET LOAF AS A BREAKFAST
OR DINNER BREAD, OR AS AN AFTERNOON SNACK WITH TEA OR COFFEE.
IT WOULD ALSO BE A WELCOME ADDITION TO A THANKSGIVING
BREAD BASKET. MILD OLIVE OIL, SOMETIMES LABELED "LIGHT," IS MILD
IN FLAVOR BUT DOES NOT HAVE FEWER CALORIES.

¾ cup yellow cornmeal

¾ cup all-purpose flour

2½ teaspoons baking powder

½ teaspoon baking soda

¼ teaspoon salt

½ teaspoon ground cinnamon

½ teaspoon ground nutmeg

½ teaspoon ground ginger

⅛ teaspoon ground allspice

⅛ teaspoon freshly ground
    black pepper

⅓ cup mild olive oil

⅓ cup packed light brown sugar

2 large eggs

1 cup plain canned solid-
    pack pumpkin

¼ cup buttermilk or plain
    low-fat yogurt

Preheat the oven to 350°F. Butter an 8½- by 4½-inch loaf pan.

In a large bowl, stir together the cornmeal, flour, baking powder, baking soda, salt, cinnamon, nutmeg, ginger, allspice, and pepper.

In a medium-size bowl, whisk together the oil, sugar, and eggs until smooth. Whisk in the pumpkin and buttermilk or yogurt.

Pour the pumpkin-egg mixture over the flour mixture and stir just until blended. Pour the batter into the prepared pan and bake for 35 to 40 minutes, or until the loaf is lightly browned, springy to the touch, and a toothpick inserted in the center comes out clean.

Cool the bread in the pan on a wire rack for about 30 minutes, then turn the bread out onto the rack to cool completely. Cut into slices to serve.

# CHILE & CHEESE CORN BREAD

THIS CORN BREAD IS DELICIOUS SERVED STILL
WARM, BUT WRAPPED WELL, IT WILL KEEP FOR A DAY OR
TWO. MOIST AND SPICY, IT IS GOOD WITH
THE GREENS & POSOLE (P. 34), FRIED CHICKEN, OR
SIMPLE SCRAMBLED EGGS FOR BRUNCH.

1¾ cups yellow cornmeal

½ cup all-purpose flour

1 tablespoon sugar

1½ teaspoons baking powder

½ teaspoon baking soda

½ teaspoon salt

¼ teaspoon freshly ground
   black pepper

1 cup buttermilk

2 large eggs

4 tablespoons (½ stick) unsalted
   butter, melted & cooled

1¼ cups shredded pepper
   Jack cheese

1 (4-ounce) can chopped mild
   green chiles, drained

¼ cup chopped green onions

1 cup frozen corn kernels

Preheat the oven to 400°F. Grease an 8-inch-square baking pan.

In a large bowl, stir together the cornmeal, flour, sugar, baking powder, baking soda, salt, and freshly ground black pepper.

In a medium-size bowl, whisk together the buttermilk, eggs, and butter. Stir in the pepper Jack cheese, green chiles, and green onions. Stir in the frozen corn kernels.

Pour the buttermilk mixture over the cornmeal mixture and stir just until blended; the batter will be wet and clumpy. Pour into the prepared pan and gently smooth the top with a spatula.

Bake for 30 to 35 minutes, or until the top and edges are lightly browned and the corn bread is firm to the touch. Transfer the pan to a wire rack and let cool until warm before cutting into 9 squares to serve.

# BLUE CORNMEAL &
# BLUEBERRY MUFFINS

MAKES 12 MUFFINS

BLUE CORNMEAL, A VARIETY WITH A SLIGHTLY
RICHER TASTE THAN YELLOW, IS SOLD IN SOME HEALTH-FOOD
SHOPS AND SPECIALTY FOOD STORES—BUT YELLOW
WORKS FINE, TOO. BEST WHEN FRESHLY BAKED, LEFTOVERS
MAY BE REHEATED OR WELL-WRAPPED AND FROZEN.

Preheat the oven to 375°F. Grease a 12-cup muffin tin or line the cups with foil liners.

In a large bowl, stir together the cornmeal, flour, baking powder, baking soda, cinnamon, salt, and allspice until well blended.

In a medium-size bowl, whisk together the eggs, sugar, and melted butter. Whisk in the yogurt, vanilla extract, and lemon zest.

Pour the egg mixture over the flour mixture and sprinkle the blueberries on top. Mix gently, until the ingredients are just incorporated. Frozen berries will make the batter very stiff and cold.

Spoon the batter into the prepared muffin cups, dividing equally (they will be very full). Bake for about 25 minutes, or until the muffins are lightly browned and spring back when gently touched. Turn the muffins out onto a rack and let cool until warm.

1½ cups blue cornmeal

1¼ cups all-purpose flour

1 tablespoon baking powder

½ teaspoon baking soda

¾ teaspoon ground cinnamon

¼ teaspoon salt

⅛ teaspoon ground allspice

2 large eggs

½ cup sugar

6 tablespoons unsalted butter, melted & cooled

¾ cup plain low-fat yogurt

1 teaspoon vanilla extract

½ teaspoon grated lemon zest

2 cups fresh or unthawed frozen blueberries

# OAT & HAZELNUT SCONES WITH APRICOTS & CARDAMOM

MAKES 14 SCONES

USE MOIST CALIFORNIA APRICOTS FOR THESE
SOPHISTICATED SCONES. IF YOUR HAZELNUTS HAVE ALREADY BEEN
PEELED, CUT THE TOASTING TIME BY A FEW MINUTES.
SCONES ARE BEST WITHIN EATEN HOURS OF COMING FROM THE OVEN,
BUT LEFTOVERS CAN BE TIGHTLY WRAPPED AND REHEATED.

1 cup hazelnuts

¾ cup old-fashioned oats

2⅓ cups all-purpose flour

1 tablespoon baking powder

½ teaspoon baking soda

1 teaspoon ground cardamom

½ teaspoon ground ginger

¼ teaspoon salt

¾ cup (1½ sticks) cold unsalted
butter, cut into small pieces

¾ cup dried apricot halves, each cut
into 6 to 8 pieces

⅔ cup buttermilk

½ cup granulated sugar

2 large eggs

1 teaspoon vanilla extract

Preheat the oven to 375°F. Generously butter two heavy baking sheets.

Put the hazelnuts in a small baking pan and toast for 13 to 16 minutes, shaking the pan several times, until they are lightly browned and fragrant. Tip the nuts into a cotton (not terry cloth) dish towel and let cool slightly. Rub the nuts through the towel to remove as much of their skins as possible. Finely chop the nuts by hand or in a food processor.

Process the oats and 1 cup of the flour in a food processor fitted with the metal blade until the oats are very finely chopped.

In a large bowl, stir together the oat and flour mixture, the remaining 1⅓ cups flour, the baking powder, baking soda, cardamom, ginger, and salt. Cut in the butter with a pastry blender until the mixture forms fine crumbs. Add the apricots and hazelnuts and toss to distribute evenly.

In a medium-size bowl, beat together the buttermilk, sugar, eggs, and vanilla extract. Pour over the dry ingredients and mix just until incorporated. Drop the dough by ⅓ cupfuls spaced about 2 inches apart on the prepared baking sheets.

Bake for 18 to 20 minutes, or until the scones are browned in spots on the top. Transfer the scones to a wire rack and let cool, loosely covered with a dish towel, until warm.

# GIANT BRAN & RAISIN MUFFINS
# WITH TOASTED WALNUTS

MAKES 6 MUFFINS

THESE MUFFINS ARE PACKED WITH RAISINS
AND WALNUTS AND SUBTLY FLAVORED WITH MOLASSES AND
GINGER. IF YOU PREFER A LESS HEFTY MUFFIN,
SPOON THE BATTER INTO A REGULAR-SIZE 12-CUP MUFFIN
TIN AND BAKE FOR A FEW MINUTES LESS.

Preheat the oven to 350°F. Butter 6 large (7 to 8 ounces each) muffin cups.

Place the walnuts in a small baking pan and toast, shaking the pan several times, for 8 to 10 minutes, or until the nuts are lightly toasted. Immediately tip the walnuts out onto a plate to stop the cooking.

Meanwhile, in a large bowl, combine the bran and milk and let stand, stirring 2 or 3 times, for 10 minutes, or until most of the milk is absorbed. With a wooden spoon, beat in the eggs, molasses, and melted butter. Stir in the raisins and toasted walnuts.

In a medium-size bowl, stir together the flours, sugar, baking powder, baking soda, cinnamon, ginger, and salt. Add the flour mixture to the bran-milk mixture and stir just until incorporated.

Spoon the batter into the prepared muffin cups, dividing equally, filling them nearly to the top. Bake for 25 to 30 minutes, or until the tops are lightly browned and the muffins are firm to the touch. Turn the muffins out onto a wire rack and let cool until warm.

¾ cup coarsely chopped walnuts

1½ cups wheat bran

1¼ cups milk

2 large eggs

⅓ cup mild unsulphured molasses

4 tablespoons (½ stick) unsalted butter, melted & cooled

⅔ cup dark seedless raisins

1 cup all-purpose flour

½ cup whole-wheat flour

1 tablespoon sugar

1 tablespoon baking powder

½ teaspoon baking soda

1 teaspoon ground cinnamon

¾ teaspoon ground ginger

¼ teaspoon salt

# FENNEL & ORANGE RYE BREAD

MAKES 2 LARGE LOAVES

THIS MOIST BREAD IS WONDERFUL
FRESH OR TOASTED, AS A SNACK TOPPED WITH
SLICES OF MILD CHEESE AND SMOKY HAM.
GRINDING THE FENNEL AND CARAWAY WITH THE FLOUR
RELEASES THE FLAVOR OF THE SEEDS.

1 (¼-ounce) package active
    dry yeast

½ teaspoon granulated sugar

1¼ cups lukewarm
    (95° to 105°F) water

2½ cups rye flour

1 tablespoon plus 1 teaspoon
    fennel seeds

1 tablespoon caraway seeds

1 cup lukewarm
    (95° to 105°F) milk

½ cup mild unsulphured molasses

2 tablespoons packed dark
    brown sugar

2 tablespoons grated orange zest

2 tablespoons olive oil or
    vegetable oil

2½ teaspoons salt

5 to 5½ cups bread flour

1 egg yolk, beaten with
    2 teaspoons milk

In a large bowl or the bowl of a heavy-duty electric mixer fitted with the paddle attachment, sprinkle the yeast and granulated sugar over ¼ cup of the warm water. Stir just until mixed and let stand for about 10 minutes, or until foamy.

Meanwhile, in a food processor fitted with the metal blade, combine the rye flour, fennel seeds, and caraway seeds and process for about 2 minutes, or until the seeds are chopped and the flour is fragrant.

To the yeast mixture, add the remaining warm water, the warm milk, molasses, brown sugar, orange zest, oil, and salt and whisk until blended. Beat in the rye flour to make a smooth batter. Beat in the bread flour, about ½ cup at a time, to make a soft, rough, slightly sticky dough. If using a mixer, switch to the dough hook after about 4 cups of flour.

Turn the dough out onto a lightly floured work surface and knead, adding flour 1 tablespoon at a time, as necessary, for 5 to 7 minutes, or until the dough is smooth, but slightly sticky and elastic. If using a dough hook, knead for 3 to 4 minutes, turn out the dough, and knead for 2 minutes by hand.

Clean and oil the mixing bowl. Place the dough in the bowl and turn it over to oil the top. Cover with a dish towel and let rise in a warm place, away from drafts, for 1 to 1½ hours, or until

doubled in volume. Butter two heavy baking sheets.

Punch down the dough. Knead on an unfloured work surface for about 30 seconds, or until smooth. Cut in half. Shape each half into an oval and press the side of your hand lengthwise into the center of the oval to make a deep crease. Bring the edges up and pinch them together. Roll the dough over so the seam is down and place on a prepared baking sheet. Repeat with the other half of the dough. Cover and let rise for 45 minutes to 1 hour, or until doubled in volume. Fifteen minutes before the loaves have fully risen, preheat the oven to 375°F.

With a sharp knife, diagonally slash the tops of each loaf in 3 places. Brush the loaves with the egg-milk mixture, taking care not to glue the dough to the pans. Bake for 40 to 45 minutes, turning the pans around halfway thorough baking, until the loaves are well browned and sound hollow when tapped on the bottom. Cool on wire racks.

# ROSEMARY & RED ONION FOCACCIA

ENJOY THIS SAVORY HERBED FLAT BREAD WARM
FROM THE OVEN OR AT LEAST THE SAME DAY IT IS
BAKED. GOOD ACCOMPANIMENTS ARE FLAVORFUL OLIVES AND
THIN SLICES OF PARMIGIANO-REGGIANO.

1 cup lukewarm
   (95° to 105°F) water

1 (¼-ounce) package active
   dry yeast

½ teaspoon sugar

3 tablespoons extra-virgin olive oil

2 teaspoons minced fresh
   rosemary leaves

1½ teaspoons coarse salt

2 cups bread flour

1 to 1¼ cups rye flour

TOPPING

1 medium-size red onion, halved
   & thinly sliced crosswise

2 tablespoons small fresh
   rosemary sprigs

2 tablespoons extra-virgin olive oil

½ teaspoon coarse salt

⅛ teaspoon freshly ground
   black pepper

Place ½ cup of the lukewarm water in a large bowl or the bowl of an electric mixer fitted with the paddle attachment. Sprinkle the yeast and sugar over the water and stir just until mixed. Let stand for about 10 minutes, or until foamy.

Stir in the remaining ½ cup lukewarm water, the oil, rosemary, and salt. With a wooden spoon or the mixer, beat in the bread flour to make a sticky, elastic batter. Beat in enough rye flour to make a slightly dense but not sticky dough.

Turn the dough out onto a work surface lightly dusted with rye flour or use the mixer's dough hook and knead for 8 to 10 minutes, or until the dough is very smooth and elastic, adding additional rye flour as needed, about 1 tablespoon at a time, to prevent sticking. If kneading with the mixer, it will take about 5 minutes.

Clean and oil the mixing bowl. Return the dough to the bowl and turn it over to oil the top. Cover with a damp dish towel and let rise in a warm place, away from drafts, for about 1½ hours, or until doubled in volume.

Butter a 13- by 9-inch baking pan. Punch down the dough. Turn it out onto a lightly floured work surface and roll or pat into a rectangle about the same size as the prepared pan. Fit the dough into the pan, pressing it into the corners; don't

worry if it doesn't fit perfectly. Cover with a dish towel and let rise in a warm place, away from drafts, for about 45 minutes, or until not quite doubled in volume; the dough will be quite thin.

Press your fingertips into the dough to dimple it all over. Cover and let rise in a warm place for 1 to 1½ hours, or until doubled in volume.

About 15 minutes before the dough has fully risen, preheat the oven to 425°F.

Add the topping: After the dough has fully risen, scatter the onion and rosemary over the top. Drizzle with the oil and sprinkle with the salt and black pepper.

Bake for 25 minutes, or until golden brown at the edges and on the underside. Lift the focaccia from the pan to a wire rack and let cool until warm. Cut into 12 squares to serve.

*Rosemary & Red Onion Focaccia (overleaf)*

# BUCKWHEAT SILVER-DOLLAR PANCAKES

THESE SAVORY PANCAKES, A COUSIN TO
YEAST-RAISED BLINI, MAKE A STYLISH APPETIZER OR FIRST
COURSE. THE TAPENADE IS BASED ON ONE FROM
GARY DANKO, EXECUTIVE CHEF OF THE RESTAURANT, AT THE
RITZ CARLTON HOTEL IN SAN FRANCISCO.

## TAPENADE

¾ cup firmly packed sun-dried
   tomato halves, not
   packed in oil

2 cups boiling water

¼ cup coarsely chopped fresh
   flat-leaf parsley

8 Calamata olives, pitted

1 tablespoon extra-virgin olive oil

2 teaspoons red wine vinegar

1 teaspoon capers, drained

1 teaspoon coarsely chopped
   canned anchovies, blotted

1 teaspoon Dijon mustard

Salt and freshly ground black
   pepper to taste

## BUCKWHEAT PANCAKES

½ cup buckwheat flour

½ cup all-purpose flour

1 teaspoon sugar

1 teaspoon baking powder

½ teaspoon baking soda

½ teaspoon plus a pinch of salt

1 cup sour cream

2 large eggs, separated

2 tablespoons extra-virgin olive oil

Olive oil, for the griddle

Sour cream and snipped fresh
   chives, for garnish

Prepare the tapenade: In a medium-size bowl, combine the sun-dried tomatoes and boiling water. Let stand for 10 to 15 minutes, or until softened. Drain the tomatoes in a colander, reserving 2 tablespoons of the soaking liquid.

In a food processor fitted with the metal blade, combine the drained tomatoes, parsley, olives, oil, vinegar, capers, anchovies, mustard, and the reserved soaking liquid and process until puréed. Scrape into a small bowl and season to taste with salt and pepper. Cover and refrigerate until ready to use, for up to 1 week.

Prepare the pancakes: In a large bowl, stir together the flours, sugar, baking powder, baking soda, and the ½ teaspoon salt until well mixed.

In a medium-size bowl, whisk together the sour cream, egg yolks, oil, and 3 tablespoons water.

In a clean medium-size bowl, with an electric mixer set at high speed, beat the egg whites with a pinch of salt just until stiff peaks form.

Pour the sour cream mixture over the flour mixture and stir just until blended. Add the egg whites and fold in with a rubber spatula until no white streaks remain.

Preheat the oven to 200°F. Place two baking sheets in the oven to hold the pancakes.

Heat a griddle or a heavy skillet over medium-low heat until it feels hot when you hold your hand above it. Brush the griddle with oil. For each pancake, drop 1 tablespoon batter onto the griddle. The batter will be thick, but do not spread it out. Cook for 1½ to 2½ minutes, or until a few bubbles appear on the surface, the edges look cooked, and the undersides are golden brown. Turn the pancakes over and cook for about 2 minutes, or until browned. Place the pancakes on the pans in the oven and continue with the remaining batter.

To serve, arrange the pancakes on warmed plates. Top each with 1 teaspoon of the tapenade and 1 teaspoon of sour cream. Sprinkle with chives and serve immediately.

# SWISS MUESLI
# WITH TOASTED CASHEWS

MUESLI, A EUROPEAN PREDECESSOR OF GRANOLA, WAS CREATED

AT THE END OF THE NINETEENTH CENTURY BY A SWISS NUTRITIONIST.

ALMONDS ARE THE NUT MOST OFTEN FOUND IN MUESLI, A

COMBINATION OF ROLLED OATS, DRIED FRUITS, AND A LITTLE SWEETENER,

BUT HERE THE CASHEWS ADD A LUXURIOUS TOUCH.

1 cup unsalted raw cashews

3 cups old-fashioned rolled oats

1 cup diced dried apples

¾ cup dried currants

½ cup toasted wheat germ

¼ cup raw unsalted sunflower seeds

¼ cup raw unsalted pumpkin seeds

¼ cup packed light brown sugar

Preheat the oven to 375°F. Lightly press the tip of a paring knife into the natural seam of each cashew and jiggle it slightly to halve each nut.

Place the cashews in a medium-size baking pan and bake, stirring several times, for 15 to 18 minutes, or until lightly toasted. Immediately tip the cashews out onto a plate to cool.

In a large bowl, toss together all the ingredients, crumbling the sugar with your fingers. Serve with milk or yogurt. Store, tightly covered, at room temperature, for up to two weeks.

# MIXED-GRAIN GRANOLA

VARY YOUR GRANOLA: CHOOSE CHOPPED SKINNED HAZELNUTS
OR PECANS INSTEAD OF ALMONDS, OR CURRANTS, CHOPPED DATES, OR
DRIED PINEAPPLE FOR THE RAISINS. FOR FRESHNESS, WHOLE-GRAIN
FLAKES SHOULD BE KEPT REFRIGERATED. IF YOU CANNOT FIND ONE OF
THE FLAKES LISTED, INCREASE THE QUANTITY OF ANOTHER.

2 cups old-fashioned oats

1½ cups barley flakes

1½ cups spelt flakes

1½ cups wheat flakes

1 cup sliced unblanched almonds

¾ cup sesame seeds

½ cup raw unsalted pumpkin seeds

⅓ cup packed light brown sugar

2 tablespoons boiling water

⅓ cup vegetable oil

⅓ cup honey

1 tablespoon vanilla extract

¼ teaspoon salt

1 cup seedless dark raisins

½ cup seedless golden raisins

Preheat the oven to 325°F.

In a large roasting pan, mix together the oats, the barley, spelt, and wheat flakes, almonds, sesame seeds, and pumpkin seeds.

Bake, stirring every 10 minutes, for 40 to 50 minutes, or until the flakes are lightly toasted and the almonds are crisp and lightly browned.

In a medium-size bowl, whisk together the brown sugar and boiling water until the sugar is dissolved. Gradually whisk in the oil, and then the honey, vanilla extract, and salt. If the mixture separates, whisk in another tablespoon of boiling water. Pour over the toasted mixture and toss with two spoons until thoroughly coated.

Bake for 15 minutes longer, stirring frequently. Transfer the pan to a wire rack to cool completely, breaking up the large chunks with a spatula. (The granola will become crisp as it cools.) Add the raisins and toss until mixed.

# CRANBERRY & APPLE CRUMBLE

SERVES 8 TO 10

A CRUMBLE CAN BE LOOSELY DESCRIBED AS BAKED FRUIT
COVERED WITH A CRUNCHY, ALMOST SHORTBREAD-LIKE TOPPING.
SELECT TART APPLES SUCH AS EMPIRE, CORTLAND,
WINESAP, OR GRANNY SMITH. IN SEASON, SLICED RHUBARB, PEACHES,
PLUMS, AND NECTARINES ARE DELICIOUS ALTERNATIVES.

Preheat the oven to 375°F.

Prepare the fruit: In an 11¾- by 7½-inch baking dish, toss together the apple wedges, cranberries, granulated sugar, lemon juice, and cinnamon and set aside.

Prepare the topping: In a large bowl, stir together the flour, oats, brown sugar, walnuts, cinnamon, and salt, crumbling the lumps of sugar with your fingers. Using your fingertips, two knives, or a pastry blender, cut in the butter until coarse crumbs form. Sprinkle the topping over the fruit.

Bake for 35 to 40 minutes, or until the apples are very tender, the juices bubbly, and the topping crisp and browned. Serve with unsweetened softly whipped cream or vanilla ice cream.

### FRUIT

5 large tart apples, peeled, cored & cut into ½-inch wedges

1½ cups fresh or unthawed frozen cranberries, picked over

6 tablespoons granulated sugar

1 tablespoon fresh lemon juice

½ teaspoon ground cinnamon

### TOPPING

1 cup all-purpose flour

¾ cup old-fashioned rolled oats

¾ cup packed dark brown sugar

¾ cup chopped walnuts

¾ teaspoon ground cinnamon

⅛ teaspoon salt

½ cup plus 2 tablespoons cold unsalted butter, cut into small pieces

*Cranberry & Apple Crumble (overleaf)*

# WHOLE-WHEAT SHORTBREAD TRIANGLES

SHORTBREAD IS OFTEN PRESSED INTO A PIE PLATE,
BAKED, AND CUT INTO THICK WEDGES, BUT THESE COOKIES ARE
THINNER AND MORE DELICATE. THE WHOLE-WHEAT
PASTRY FLOUR MAKES A TENDER COOKIE BECAUSE IT HAS A LOWER
GLUTEN CONTENT THAN REGULAR WHOLE-WHEAT FLOUR.

¾ cup pecans

⅓ cup granulated sugar

1 cup (2 sticks) lightly salted
butter, at room temperature

¼ cup packed light brown sugar

1 teaspoon vanilla extract

¼ teaspoon salt

1½ cups whole-wheat pastry flour

½ cup all-purpose flour

3 tablespoons cornstarch

Preheat the oven to 325°F. Place the pecans in a small baking pan and bake, shaking the pan several times, for 10 to 15 minutes, or until the nuts are toasted. Transfer the nuts to a plate and cool slightly. Leave the oven at 325°F.

In a food processor fitted with the metal blade, combine the nuts and 2 tablespoons granulated sugar and process until the mixture is very finely chopped, but not oily.

In the bowl of an electric mixer, at medium-high speed, beat together the butter, brown sugar, remaining granulated sugar, vanilla, and salt until light and creamy, scraping the bowl as needed.

In a medium-size bowl, stir together the flours and cornstarch. Stir in the pecans. Add the flour mixture to the creamed mixture all at once and mix on low until the dough starts to come together. Scrape down the side of the bowl and finish mixing with a spoon. The dough will be crumbly.

Lightly dust a work surface with all-purpose flour. Knead the dough on the floured surface two or three times, just until it forms a fairly smooth ball. Flatten the dough into a disk and cut in half. Wrap half the dough in plastic wrap and refrigerate.

Place the other half of the dough between two sheets of waxed paper and roll into an 8½-inch square, about ¼-inch-thick. Remove the top sheet

of paper and trim the dough to a neat 8-inch square. Cut the dough into 5 strips, each 1½ inches wide. Cut each strip diagonally across into 7 triangles. With a thin floured metal spatula, lift the triangles to heavy ungreased baking sheets, spacing them about 1 inch apart. Gather scraps together, roll out, and cut as above.

Bake the cookies for 10 to 13 minutes, or just until the edges start to brown lightly. Let them cool on the sheets for 2 minutes, then transfer to wire racks to cool completely. Repeat with the remaining dough.

# SWEET GRITS PUDDING WITH FRESH ORANGE-CARAMEL TOPPING

SERVES 8

THIS RECIPE MAY BE CONTRARY TO
SOUTHERN TRADITION (IN THE SOUTH, GRITS ARE NEVER
SERVED WITH SUGAR), BUT YANKEES LOVE
THIS PUDDING, INSPIRED BY A CHILDHOOD FAVORITE,
TAPIOCA WITH CHOPPED FRESH ORANGES.

2¼ cups milk

½ vanilla bean, split-lengthwise

⅛ teaspoon salt

¾ cup old-fashioned grits

½ cup heavy cream

¼ cup granulated sugar

ORANGE-CARAMEL
TOPPING

5 medium-size navel oranges,
peel & pith removed

3 tablespoons packed dark
brown sugar

In a heavy large nonreactive saucepan, combine 2 cups milk and the vanilla bean. Place over medium-high heat just until small bubbles appear around the edge of the pan. Remove from the heat, cover, and steep for 20 minutes. Remove the vanilla bean and scrape the seeds with the tip of a paring knife into the milk.

Add 2 cups water and the salt to the milk and bring to a boil over medium-high heat. Add the grits in a slow, steady stream, whisking constantly. Reduce the heat to low, cover, and cook, stirring frequently and vigorously with a wooden spoon, for 25 to 30 minutes, or until the grits are very thick and creamy and have lost their uncooked taste.

Remove the mixture from the heat and stir in the cream, granulated sugar, and the remaining ¼ cup milk. Spoon into a serving dish, cover, and chill for at least 3 hours.

Meanwhile, prepare the topping: With a serrated knife, working over a bowl to catch the juices, cut out the sections from the orange membranes. Set the sections aside on a plate. Squeeze the juice from the membranes into the bowl.

Stir the brown sugar into the orange juice until the sugar is dissolved. Add the orange sections and toss to mix. Cover and chill. Serve the orange topping over the pudding.

# LEMON & ROSEMARY
# CORNMEAL COOKIES

MAKES ABOUT 3 1/2 DOZEN COOKIES

ROSEMARY ADDS A SAVORY ACCENT THAT MAKES THESE
SWEET TEACAKES A FINE PARTNER TO DESSERT WINE OR ESPRESSO.
THE RECIPE WAS INSPIRED BY ONE IN RICHARD SAX'S BOOK,
*CLASSIC HOME DESSERTS*. THEY WILL KEEP FOR UP TO TWO DAYS IN A
TIGHTLY COVERED TIN AT ROOM TEMPERATURE.

¾ cup seedless golden raisins

¼ cup dark rum

1 very large lemon

¾ cup sugar

1¼ teaspoons dried rosemary

¾ cup (1½ sticks) unsalted butter,
    at room temperature

¼ teaspoon salt

2 large eggs, at room temperature

1 teaspoon vanilla extract

1¼ cups all-purpose flour

1 cup yellow cornmeal

1½ teaspoons baking powder

In a small bowl, soak the raisins in the rum for at least 2 hours or overnight. Drain.

With a swivel-blade vegetable peeler, remove the zest from the lemon in large strips to get a scant ¼ cup. In a food processor fitted with the metal blade, combine the sugar and lemon zest and process for about 2 minutes, or until the peel is finely chopped and the sugar is quite damp. Add the rosemary, scrape down the side of the work bowl, and process for about 1 minute longer, or until some of the rosemary leaves are broken up and combined with the sugar.

Transfer the sugar to the bowl of an electric mixer. Add the butter and salt and, at medium-high speed, beat until light and fluffy. Add the eggs, 1 at a time, and beat until well blended. Beat in the vanilla extract. Scrape down the side of the bowl.

At low speed, mix in the flour until partially mixed in. The batter will be very clumpy and the flour will still be visible along the side of the bowl. Add the cornmeal and baking powder and mix until almost blended. By hand, stir in the raisins until all the ingredients are incorporated. Cover and chill the dough for at least 1 hour, or until firm but not rock hard. (If the dough gets too hard, let it soften at room temperature for 20 minutes or so.)

Preheat the oven to 350°F. Butter several heavy baking sheets.

With lightly floured hands, pull off small pieces of dough, measuring about 1 tablespoon each, and roll into rough 1-inch balls, reflouring your hands as needed. Place 2 inches apart on the prepared baking sheets.

Bake for 9 to 12 minutes, or until the edges just begin to brown. With a metal spatula, immediately transfer to wire racks to cool.

# OAT BRAN, BANANA &
# CHOCOLATE CHIP LOAF

THIS LOAF TASTES BEST THE DAY AFTER BAKING.
FOR THE MOST INTENSE BANANA FLAVOR, USE BANANAS THAT ARE
VERY RIPE AND BLACK—AT THE POINT WHEN YOU ARE
ALMOST READY TO THROW THEM OUT. IF YOU CAN'T FIND MINIATURE
CHOCOLATE CHIPS, USE REGULAR-SIZE AND CHOP THEM UP.

1¼ cups all-purpose flour

¾ cup oat bran

½ cup whole-wheat flour

1½ teaspoons baking powder

½ teaspoon baking soda

¼ teaspoon salt

1 cup sugar

2 large eggs, at room temperature

4 tablespoons (½ stick) unsalted
butter, melted & cooled

1 teaspoon vanilla extract

1 cup mashed ripe banana
(about 2 large bananas)

½ cup light sour cream

½ cup miniature semisweet
chocolate chips

Preheat the oven to 325°F. Butter a 9- by 5- by 3-inch loaf pan.

In a medium-size bowl, stir together the all-purpose flour, oat bran, whole-wheat flour, baking powder, baking soda, and salt.

In a large bowl, whisk together the sugar, eggs, butter, and vanilla extract until smooth and light in color. Whisk in the mashed banana and sour cream.

Add the flour mixture to the banana mixture and stir just until incorporated. The batter will be gritty because of the oat bran. Stir in the chocolate chips. Scrape the batter into the prepared pan and smooth the top.

Bake for 55 to 60 minutes, or until the loaf is well browned, has shrunk from the sides of the pan, and a toothpick inserted just off center comes out with moist but not wet crumbs adhering to it. (The center may sink slightly.) Transfer the pan to a wire rack to cool for 30 minutes. Loosen the edges with a thin metal spatula and invert onto the rack. Turn over and cool completely.

Cut into slices to serve.

# INDEX

# CONVERSION TABLE

## WEIGHTS

| ounces & pounds | metric equivalents |
|---|---|
| ¼ ounce | 7 grams |
| ⅓ ounce | 10 g |
| ½ ounce | 14 g |
| 1 ounce | 28 g |
| 1½ ounces | 42 g |
| 1¾ ounces | 50 g |
| 2 ounces | 57 g |
| 3 ounces | 85 g |
| 3½ ounces | 100 g |
| 4 ounces (¼ pound) | 114 g |
| 6 ounces | 170 g |
| 8 ounces (½ pound) | 227 g |
| 9 ounces | 250 g |
| 16 ounces (1 pound) | 464 g |

## TEMPERATURES

| °F (Fahrenheit) | °C (Celsius or Centigrade) |
|---|---|
| 32 (water freezes) | 0 |
| 200 | 93.3 |
| 212 (water boils) | 100 |
| 250 | 120 |
| 275 | 135 |
| 300 (slow oven) | 150 |
| 325 | 160 |
| 350 (moderate oven) | 175 |
| 375 | 190 |
| 400 (hot oven) | 205 |
| 425 | 220 |
| 450 (very hot oven) | 233 |
| 475 | 245 |
| 500 (extremely hot oven) | 260 |

## LIQUID MEASURES

| spoons & cups | metric equivalents |
|---|---|
| ¼ teaspoon | 1.23 mm |
| ½ teaspoon | 2.5 mm |
| ¾ teaspoon | 3.7 mm |
| 1 teaspoon | 5 mm |
| 1 dessertspoon | 10 mm |
| 1 tablespoon (3 teaspoons) | 15 mm |
| 2 tablespoons (1 ounce) | 30 mm |
| ¼ cup | 60 mm |
| ⅓ cup | 80 mm |
| ½ cup | 120 mm |
| ⅔ cup | 160 mm |
| ¾ cup | 180 mm |
| 1 cup (8 ounces) | 240 mm |
| 2 cups (1 pint) | 480 mm |
| 3 cups | 710 mm |
| 4 cups (1 quart) | 1 liter |
| 4 quarts (1 gallon) | 3¾ liters |

## LENGTH

| U.S. measurements | metric equivalents |
|---|---|
| ⅛ inch | 3 mm |
| ¼ inch | 6 mm |
| ⅜ inch | 1 cm |
| ½ inch | 1.2 cm |
| ¾ inch | 2 cm |
| 1 inch | 2.5 cm |
| 1¼ inches | 3.1 cm |
| 1½ inches | 3.7 cm |
| 2 inches | 5 cm |
| 3 inches | 7.5 cm |
| 4 inches | 10 cm |
| 5 inches | 12.5 cm |

## APPROXIMATE EQUIVALENTS

1 kilo is slightly more than 2 pounds
1 liter is slightly more than 1 quart
1 meter is slightly over 3 feet
1 centimeter is approximately ⅜ inch